THE BELIEVER'S HANDBOOK FOR QUR'AN MEMORIZATION

The Believer's Handbook for Qur'an Memorization
by Muhammad Ibn James Sutton
First Edition
Published by Ilmstitute Academy, ilmstitute.com
Copyright © 2024/1446, Muhammad Ibn James Sutton

ISBN: 9798343813708

All rights reserved. No portion of this book may be reproduced in any form without permission from the publisher, except as permitted by U.S. copyright law. For permissions contact: ilmstitute@gmail.com.

Cover design and typesetting by ihsaandesign.com.
Printed by Amazon KDP

THE BELIEVER'S HANDBOOK FOR QUR'AN MEMORIZATION

by

Muhammad Ibn James Sutton

CONTENTS

INTRODUCTION 7

CHAPTER ONE: Why is it Important to Memorize the Quran? 12

CHAPTER TWO: Habits One Needs to Develop to Memorize
the Quran 25
    Habit 1   25
    Habit 2   27
    Habit 3   29
    Habit 4   32
    Habit 5   32
    Habit 6   37
    Habit 7   39
    Habit 8   39

CHAPTER THREE: Actions Which Will Assist You During
Your Memorization 41
    Action 1: Learn the Arabic Language   41
    Action 2: Reading Books of *Tafseer*   45
        Other books which will assist your memorization journey   46
    Action 3: Listening to the Quran   47
    Action 4: Keep a Journal   49
    Action 5: Find a Companion to Memorize and Revise with   50
    Action 6: Writing the Quran in Notebooks   51
    Action 7: Write Out a Daily Checklist   52

CHAPTER FOUR: The Best Method of Memorization 54

Contents

CHAPTER FIVE: Getting Started: The Plan 59
    Phase 1   60
    Phase 2   64
    Phase 3   66
    Phase 4   67
    Phase 5   71
    Phase 6   74
    Phase 7   76

CHAPTER SIX: Statements of the *Salaf* Regarding the Importance of Memorizing and Understanding the Quran 80

CONCLUSION 87

INTRODUCTION

إن الحمد لله نحمده ونستعينه ونستغفره ونعوذ بالله من شرور أنفسنا ومن سيئات أعمالنا من يهده الله فلا مضل له ومن يضلل فلا هادئ له وأشهد أن لا إله إلا الله وحده لا شريك له وأشهد أن محمدا عبده و رسوله صلى الله عليه وسلم .

All praise is due to Allah. We praise him, we seek His help, we seek His forgiveness, and we seek refuge in Allah from the evil within ourselves and our evil deeds. Whoever Allah guides, there is none to misguide him. Whoever Allah leaves to stray, there is none to guide him. I testify there is no God worthy of worship except Allah alone, without any partners, and that Muhammad, peace and blessings be upon him, is His servant and His messenger.

﴿ يَٰٓأَيُّهَا ٱلَّذِينَ ءَامَنُوا۟ ٱتَّقُوا۟ ٱللَّهَ حَقَّ تُقَاتِهِۦ وَلَا تَمُوتُنَّ إِلَّا وَأَنتُم مُّسْلِمُونَ ﴾

O you who have faith, fear Allah as it is His right to be feared and do not die unless you are Muslims. (3:102)

﴿ يَٰٓأَيُّهَا ٱلنَّاسُ ٱتَّقُوا۟ رَبَّكُمُ ٱلَّذِى خَلَقَكُم مِّن نَّفْسٍ وَٰحِدَةٍ وَخَلَقَ مِنْهَا زَوْجَهَا وَبَثَّ مِنْهُمَا رِجَالًا كَثِيرًا وَنِسَآءً ۚ وَٱتَّقُوا۟ ٱللَّهَ ٱلَّذِى تَسَآءَلُونَ بِهِۦ وَٱلْأَرْحَامَ ۚ إِنَّ ٱللَّهَ كَانَ عَلَيْكُمْ رَقِيبًا ﴾

O humanity! Be mindful of your Lord Who created you from a single soul, and from it He created its mate, and through both He spread countless men and women. And be mindful of Allah—in Whose Name you appeal to one another—and honour family ties. Surely Allah is ever Watchful over you. (4:1)

Introduction

$$\text{يَا أَيُّهَا الَّذِينَ آمَنُوا اتَّقُوا اللَّهَ وَقُولُوا قَوْلًا سَدِيدًا ۞ يُصْلِحْ لَكُمْ أَعْمَالَكُمْ وَيَغْفِرْ لَكُمْ ذُنُوبَكُمْ ۗ وَمَن يُطِعِ اللَّهَ وَرَسُولَهُ فَقَدْ فَازَ فَوْزًا عَظِيمًا ۞}$$

Fear Allah and speak words as befitting. He will amend your deeds for you and forgive your sins. Whoever obeys Allah and His messenger has achieved a great triumph. (33:70-71)

أما بعد: فإن أصدق الحديث كتاب الله، وخير الهدي هدي محمد صلى الله عليه وسلم، شر الأمور محدثاتها، وكل محدثة بدعة، وكل بدعة ضلالة، وكل ضلالة في النار. ثم أما بعد:

The truest of all speech is the Book of Allah, and the best guidance is the guidance of Muhammad. The evilest matters are those that are newly invented matters in the religion, for every newly invented matter is an innovation. Every innovation is misguidance, and every misguidance is in the Hellfire. To proceed...

The idea to undertake this project stemmed from my previous book *The Believer's Handbook for Seeking Knowledge*. In that book, I dedicated an entire section to the memorization of the Quran. However, I did not have the space to go into the detail that I wanted to go into. The topic of memorizing the Quran and how one should memorize the Quran cannot be summed up in a small chapter.

Upon completion of my previous book, I made it my intention to one day sit down and expand on that chapter about memorization of the Quran, so my ideas and the plan I laid out for the people would become clear. I was not able to begin the project I wanted because I took a position as an Imam in Fresno, California, which caused me to become busy with classes and issues pertaining to the Masjid. Now that my schedule has sort of become regulated, I am using the bit of free time I have to carry out my original intention *insha'Allah*.

Memorizing the Quran is a very important issue for me as I am sure it is for a lot of Muslims. I left America in November of 2000 to go

Introduction

to Yemen with the sole purpose of memorizing the Quran and learning the Arabic language. I did not know about all the different sciences that I would be studying because I was still young and naïve. I also was not aware of the lack of stability that Yemen constantly experiences that would cause many ups and downs in my ability to get the things done that I needed to get done.

In July of 2001, Shaykh Muqbil died in Saudi Arabia, and that caused a lot of fear to ripple through the different groups of foreigners studying in Dammaj. By the time the Shaykh died, I had memorized the last three *Juz* of the Quran, I finished *Surah Al-Baqarah*, and I was working on *Surah Ali Imran*. I was moving along towards my goal. However, the death of the Shaykh brought with it rumors of the government coming in and kicking us all out of Yemen. Shaykh Muqbil's successor, Shaykh Yahya ibn Ali Al-Hajoori, knew of these rumors and knew of the fear of the foreigners, so one day he decided to advise us.

Shaykh Yahya told us all to focus on taking the lessons and to put memorizing the Quran on hold. He told us,

> It is more important that you can go back to the people and teach them. You need knowledge for that. The people need more people that can teach them, not just lead them in *Salat*. You can finish memorizing the Quran when you go back to teach your people.

I ended up taking his advice. I did not stop memorizing completely, but I was not memorizing at the pace that I was before. I would bounce around between reading the Quran a lot and memorizing. I would sit down for months at a time just reading the Quran over and over, and other times I would focus on revising and memorizing a few more *Surahs*.

In July of 2004 the first houthi war started in Sa'dah right outside of Dammaj, and Yemen was never the same from that time forward. After the first war finished, I decided to act on the advice from Shaykh Ahmed Al-Wassabi and go to Sanaa to get married. While I was in Sanaa, I continued to act on the advice of Shaykh Yahya also, and wherever I could find some classes to benefit from, I would do so. However, I got caught up in the whims of the *dunya* just like most people. I had to get my paperwork correct to become legal in the country, so I could get married. That took me about three years. During that time, a brother I was close to, Qayyim Al-Faransi, was killed by the houthis one night while he was on guard duty on the mountain. This pointed to the coming problems that were inevitable between the Students of Dammaj and the houthis. It is also pointed to the continuing instability of the country. Between the stress of trying to get my paperwork done to get married and these events, you would probably guess that I did not get much done as far as knowledge is concerned.

During these times I was struggling just to retain what I had already memorized. By the time I got married, I had to revise *Juz Amma* because what I memorized had become so weak. This is the reality that a lot of people live in. They want to memorize the Quran, but they get caught up in all the chaos of day-to-day living. The desire might be there, but the time and peace of mind, which are important to memorizing, are not there.

Once I got married, and my life started to settle down a bit, I began to formulate a plan to continue my studies, reading, and memorizing while taking care of a wife pregnant with twins with all the chaos that was about to begin in Yemen. This plan started then, and eventually developed into the plan that you will see in this book over two decades after I started the journey.

This journey does not stop with this book. This journey continues until my body is hidden in the ground. That is my mentality, *alhamdulillah*, and that should be the mentality of every person that wishes to benefit from their time on this earth.

In my early days of studying, I was always trying to race people. This caused me to be in a hurry to memorize this and that. We do not benefit in this manner. Our struggle has always been and will always be against ourselves. The struggle to discipline yourself to memorize when you do not want to. The struggle to go to the Masjid when you want to sit around and be lazy. The struggle to read the portion of the Quran

Introduction

you have to read that day instead of procrastinating. It is an ongoing struggle for us all. That is why this book is being written.

This book is not written for the person that can sit down and memorize three pages from the Quran in an hour. This book is written for the person that has to struggle to memorize every *Ayah* from the Quran which he memorizes. This book is for the man that is working to take care of his family, but he still has a desire to memorize the Quran. This book is for the man who got the bad grades in school, so the teachers dealt with him like he was stupid even though he was never stupid; he was just bored.

This book, however, is not written for the lazy person who is not ready to put in the work. If you want to memorize 604 pages and retain everything on those pages, you have to be ready to expend energy and effort you never knew you had. This journey will strengthen you *insha'Allah*. This journey will change your character for the better *insha'Allah*. This journey will change your life *insha'Allah* for the better. So, let's get started.

Muhammad Ibn James Sutton
Rabi' Ath-Thani 4, 1446 / October 7, 2024
Fresno, California

CHAPTER 1:
Why Is It Important to Memorize the Quran?

It is amazing that people would ask this question after they spent their entire lives placing importance on memorizing music. It is just natural that a person memorizes that which he places the most importance on. If a person loves music, he memorizes lyrics. If a person loves poetry, he memorizes his favorite poems. The fact that most Muslims are not concerned with memorizing Quran shows the lack of importance placed on the Quran. A sad reality it is indeed!

Allah said in the Quran:

﴿بَلْ هُوَ ءَايَـٰتٌۢ بَيِّنَـٰتٌ فِى صُدُورِ ٱلَّذِينَ أُوتُوا۟ ٱلْعِلْمَ ۚ وَمَا يَجْحَدُ بِـَٔايَـٰتِنَآ إِلَّا ٱلظَّـٰلِمُونَ﴾

But this Quran is a set of clear revelations preserved in the hearts of those gifted with knowledge. And none denies Our revelations except the stubborn wrongdoers. [29:49]

Here Allah clearly stated that the Quran is preserved in the chests of the people that He has gifted with knowledge. The preservation in the chest is through the memorization of the Quran. The knowledge that was given to them was the understanding of the Quran. This is an amazing blessing from Allah if He blesses any one of us to memorize His speech and retain it in our hearts.

1. Why is it Important to Memorize the Quran?

Memorization of the Quran was the method of revelation. Jibreel would descend to the Messenger of Allah ﷺ, recite the revelation to him, and the Prophet ﷺ would memorize what was recited to him. This can be seen in the following *Ayahs* from the Quran:

﴿لَا تُحَرِّكْ بِهِ لِسَانَكَ لِتَعْجَلَ بِهِ * إِنَّ عَلَيْنَا جَمْعَهُ وَقُرْآنَهُ * فَإِذَا قَرَأْنَاهُ فَاتَّبِعْ قُرْآنَهُ * ثُمَّ إِنَّ عَلَيْنَا بَيَانَهُ﴾

Do not rush your tongue trying to memorize a revelation of the Quran. It is certainly upon Us to make you memorize and recite it. So, once We have recited a revelation, follow its recitation closely. Then it is surely upon Us to make it clear to you. [75:16-19]

This was the method which Allah chose for His final revelation to the Prophet Muhammad ﷺ, and this method has become an Islamic tradition that has distinguished us from all the people that came before us. Each Muslim who sits down to memorize the Quran is taking part in carrying on this fine tradition.

When Imam At-Tabri gave the interpretation of the second *Ayah* that was mentioned, he said:

يقول تعالى: إن علينا جمع هذا القرآن في صدرك يا محمد حتى نثبته فيه.

Allah the Most High says: it is upon Us to bring together the Quran in your chest O Muhammad, so We can establish it in your heart.

We strive to follow the path of the Final Messenger to Mankind, Muhammad ibn Abdullah ﷺ, by memorizing and seeking the understanding of the Quran.

One of the greatest blessings Allah has given us with this Quran is that He made it easy to be read and easy to be understood. This is for our benefit, so we can read with ease what we need to be successful in this life and the next. Allah said in the Quran:

﴿وَلَقَدْ يَسَّرْنَا الْقُرْآنَ لِلذِّكْرِ فَهَلْ مِن مُّدَّكِرٍ﴾

1. Why is it Important to Memorize the Quran?

And We have certainly made the Quran easy to remember. So, is there anyone who will be mindful? [54:22]

Imam At-Tabri mentioned about this Ayah:

يقول تعالى: ولقد سهلنا القرآن وهوّناه لمن أراد التذكر به والاتعاظ

Allah the Most High said: We have made the Quran easy (for recitation and memorization), and We have facilitated the pondering of the Quran and provided lessons for those who wish to benefit from them.

We should take advantage of the ease which has been given to us by our Creator and Sustainer. We find ease in reading the Quran, ease in memorizing the Quran, and ease in understanding the Quran, but we choose to give our attention to so many other things other than the Quran. Allah warned us from turning our backs on this Quran and warned us of the consequences when He said:

﴿وَمَنْ أَعْرَضَ عَن ذِكْرِى فَإِنَّ لَهُۥ مَعِيشَةً ضَنكًا وَنَحْشُرُهُۥ يَوْمَ ٱلْقِيَـٰمَةِ أَعْمَىٰ﴾

But whoever turns away from My Reminder will certainly have a miserable life, then We will raise them up blind on the Day of Judgment. [20:24]

This *Ayah* includes all the Revelation that was sent down to Allah's Messenger ﷺ in the Quran and in the Sunnah. Turning away from the Quran, from reading the Quran, from pondering the Quran, and from acting upon the Quran will cause nothing but misery in the life of the person who chooses to do so. The person's life will become full of stress and useless distractions. The Prophet ﷺ mentioned in an authentic Hadith in *Sunan At-Tirmidhi*:

عَنْ أَبِي هُرَيْرَةَ رضي الله عنه عَنِ النَّبِيِّ ﷺ قَالَ: إِنَّ اللَّهَ تَعَالَى يَقُولُ: يَا ابْنَ آدَمَ تَفَرَّغْ لِعِبَادَتِي أَمْلَأْ صَدْرَكَ غِنًى وَأَسُدَّ فَقْرَكَ وَإِلَّا تَفْعَلْ مَلَأْتُ

1. Why is it Important to Memorize the Quran?

يَدَيْكَ شُغْلاً وَلَمْ أَسُدَّ فَقْرَكَ.

Abu Hurairah ﷺ narrated that the Messenger of Allah ﷺ said: "Indeed Allah, the Most High said: 'O son of Adam! Devote yourself to My worship, I will fill your chest with riches and alleviate your poverty. And if you do not do so, then I will fill your hands with distractions and not alleviate your poverty.'"

Therefore, we must choose to busy ourselves with that which brings us benefit in this life and the next. We must choose to busy ourselves with that which brings us closer to Allah. This starts with the Quran.

Another benefit of memorizing the Quran is that it is a source of elevation in status in this life and the next for the one that does it properly. This can be seen from a statement of Umar Ibn Al-Khattab that was narrated in *Muslim*:

عن عمر بن الخطاب ﷺ أن النبي ﷺ قال: إن الله يرفع بهذا الكتاب أقوامًا ويضع به آخرين.

'Umar bin Al-Khattab ﷺ reported: The Prophet ﷺ said, "Verily, Allah elevates some people with this Qur'an and abases others."

Allah elevates those that read the Quran, study the Quran seeking to understand it, and act on the Quran, while He abases those who turn their backs on the Quran. Allah mentioned those individuals that turned their backs on the Revelation to go after the dunya and the life of this world:

﴿وَٱتْلُ عَلَيْهِمْ نَبَأَ ٱلَّذِىٓ ءَاتَيْنَٰهُ ءَايَٰتِنَا فَٱنسَلَخَ مِنْهَا فَأَتْبَعَهُ ٱلشَّيْطَٰنُ فَكَانَ مِنَ ٱلْغَاوِينَ ۞ وَلَوْ شِئْنَا لَرَفَعْنَٰهُ بِهَا وَلَٰكِنَّهُۥٓ أَخْلَدَ إِلَى ٱلْأَرْضِ وَٱتَّبَعَ هَوَىٰهُ ۚ فَمَثَلُهُۥ كَمَثَلِ ٱلْكَلْبِ إِن تَحْمِلْ عَلَيْهِ يَلْهَثْ أَوْ تَتْرُكْهُ يَلْهَث ۚ ذَّٰلِكَ مَثَلُ ٱلْقَوْمِ ٱلَّذِينَ كَذَّبُوا۟ بِـَٔايَٰتِنَا ۚ فَٱقْصُصِ ٱلْقَصَصَ لَعَلَّهُمْ يَتَفَكَّرُونَ ۞ سَآءَ مَثَلًا ٱلْقَوْمُ ٱلَّذِينَ كَذَّبُوا۟ بِـَٔايَٰتِنَا وَأَنفُسَهُمْ كَانُوا۟ يَظْلِمُونَ﴾

And relate to them O Prophet the story of the one to

1. Why is it Important to Memorize the Quran?

whom We gave Our signs, but he abandoned them, so shaytan took hold of him, and he became a deviant. If We had willed, We would have elevated him with Our signs, but he clung to this life—following his evil desires. His example is that of a dog; if you chase it away, it pants, and if you leave it, it pants. This is the example of the people who deny Our signs. So, narrate to them stories of the past, so perhaps they will reflect. [7:175-177]

Allah clearly stated in this *Ayah* that if He had willed, He would have elevated them in status with the Revelation. This would be through Allah giving them the *Tawfeeq* to obey Him by carrying out His commands and refraining from His prohibitions. Allah sent down a true guidance to mankind to bring them out of the darkness into the light and bring them out of a state of immorality to a state of morality. Allah said in the Quran:

﴿إِنَّ هَـٰذَا ٱلْقُرْءَانَ يَهْدِى لِلَّتِى هِىَ أَقْوَمُ وَيُبَشِّرُ ٱلْمُؤْمِنِينَ ٱلَّذِينَ يَعْمَلُونَ ٱلصَّـٰلِحَـٰتِ أَنَّ لَهُمْ أَجْرًا كَبِيرًا﴾

Surely this Quran guides to what is most upright, and gives good news to the believers, who do good deeds, that they will have a mighty reward. [17:9]

The Quran guides the people to the best behavior, the best manners, the best character, and the best morals. However, this is through reading, memorizing, understanding, and implementing.

Also, in the previous *Ayah* from *Surah Al-A'raf*, Allah compared the people that turn away from the Revelation to dogs. Allah gave the example of a dog panting regardless of his chasing him away or leaving him alone. This *Ayah* means that if you bring them the *Ayaat* warning them of the punishment or if you just leave them alone, they will not listen nor change their behavior. Basically, the Quran benefits those

1. Why is it Important to Memorize the Quran?

individuals nothing.

Allah also mentioned that the reason for their turning away from the Revelation was due to their infatuation with the life of this world and their forgetting the next life. This happens when a person begins neglecting his responsibilities to Allah while focusing all his attention on what he deems are his responsibilities to the creation. He will strive to fulfill the rights people have over him and work to please the people with the hope of getting some worldly benefit for doing so while simultaneously ignoring the rights Allah has over him and showing no concern for those rights.

Another benefit for memorizing the Quran is the mercy which one will receive for doing so. Allah mentioned in the Quran:

﴿وَإِذَا قُرِئَ ٱلۡقُرۡءَانُ فَٱسۡتَمِعُواْ لَهُۥ وَأَنصِتُواْ لَعَلَّكُمۡ تُرۡحَمُونَ﴾

When the Quran is recited, listen to it attentively and be silent, so you may be shown mercy. [7:204]

In this Ayah, Allah mentioned that mercy will be shown to the person who listens attentively while remaining silent during the recitation of the Quran in the *Salat*, so what about the person who reads, memorizes, studies, and implements the Quran in his daily life? The Quran is a mercy, and the person that busies himself with the Quran will receive mercy *insha'Allah*. We can also see this in the following Hadith from *Sahih Muslim*:

عَنْ أَبِي هُرَيْرَةَ ﷺ عَنِ النَّبِيِّ ﷺ قَالَ: مَنْ نَفَّسَ عَنْ مُؤْمِنٍ كُرْبَةً مِنْ كُرَبِ الدُّنْيَا نَفَّسَ اللهُ عَنْهُ كُرْبَةً مِنْ كُرَبِ يَوْمِ الْقِيَامَةِ، وَمَنْ يَسَّرَ عَلَى مُعْسِرٍ، يَسَّرَ اللهُ عَلَيْهِ فِي الدُّنْيَا وَالْآخِرَةِ، وَمَنْ سَتَرَ مُسْلِمًا سَتَرَهُ اللهُ فِي الدُّنْيَا وَالْآخِرَةِ، وَاللهُ فِي عَوْنِ الْعَبْدِ مَا كَانَ الْعَبْدُ فِي عَوْنِ أَخِيهِ، وَمَنْ سَلَكَ طَرِيقًا يَلْتَمِسُ فِيهِ عِلْمًا سَهَّلَ اللهُ لَهُ بِهِ طَرِيقًا إِلَى الْجَنَّةِ، وَمَا اجْتَمَعَ قَوْمٌ فِي بَيْتٍ مِنْ بُيُوتِ اللهِ يَتْلُونَ كِتَابَ اللهِ، وَيَتَدَارَسُونَهُ فِيمَا بَيْنَهُمْ؛ إِلَّا نَزَلَتْ عَلَيْهِمُ السَّكِينَةُ، وَغَشِيَتْهُمُ الرَّحْمَةُ، وَحَفَّتْهُمُ الْمَلَائِكَةُ،

1. Why is it Important to Memorize the Quran?

وَذَكَرَهُمُ اللَّهُ فِيمَنْ عِنْدَهُ، وَمَنْ أَبْطَأَ بِهِ عَمَلُهُ لَمْ يُسْرِعْ بِهِ نَسَبُهُ.

Abu Hurayrah ﷺ reported: The Prophet ﷺ said: Whoever removes a worldly grief from a believer, Allah will remove from him one of the griefs of the Day of Resurrection. And whoever alleviates a debt of a person unable to repay it, Allah will alleviate his needs in this world and the Hereafter. Whoever covers the faults of a Muslim, Allah will cover his faults in this world and the Hereafter. And Allah will aid His slave so long as he aids his brother. And whoever follows a path to seek knowledge therein, Allah will make easy for him a path to Paradise. No people gather together in one of the Houses of Allah, reciting the Book of Allah and studying it among themselves, except that sakeenah (tranquility) descends upon them, and mercy envelops them, and the angels surround them, and Allah mentions them among those who are with Him. And whoever is slowed down by his actions, will not be hastened forward by his lineage.

The reward mentioned in this Hadith for sitting in the Masjid, reciting the Quran, and studying the Quran is worth striving for. People strive their entire lives in this *dunya* trying to be mentioned by a person they look up to or admire. They do everything they can to impress a specific person just to have that person notice them. In this Hadith, the Messenger ﷺ mentioned the actions we can do to be mentioned by Allah in the highest of gatherings. Is that not worth striving for? Is that not worth losing sleep over? Is that not worth giving up your desires for? May Allah guide us!

These are the people that seek to be those mentioned by Allah in the Quran:

﴿ ٱلَّذِينَ ءَاتَيْنَٰهُمُ ٱلْكِتَٰبَ يَتْلُونَهُۥ حَقَّ تِلَاوَتِهِۦٓ أُو۟لَٰٓئِكَ يُؤْمِنُونَ بِهِۦ وَمَن يَكْفُرْ بِهِۦ فَأُو۟لَٰٓئِكَ هُمُ ٱلْخَٰسِرُونَ ﴾

Those We have given the Book follow it as it should be followed. It is they who truly believe in it. As for those who reject it, it is they who are the losers. [2:121]

The word Allah used in this *Ayah* is يتلو which means to recite. A lot

1. Why is it Important to Memorize the Quran?

of people who read this *Ayah* without referring back to the Tafseer will think the *Ayah* is speaking about rules of *Tajweed*. If you were to translate it literally, it would read, "Those whom We have given the Book, they recite it the way it should be recited." However, that is not what is being referred to here. The way it should be recited is that a person should act on what he reads. If he reads a command in the Quran, he should carry it out to the best of his ability. If he reads a prohibition in the Quran, he should completely refrain from it.

The people that read the Quran in this manner are the people that are referred to in the following Hadith from *Sunan Ibn Majah*:

عَنْ أَنَسِ بْنِ مَالِكٍ ﷺ، قَالَ: قَالَ رَسُولُ اللَّهِ ﷺ: إِنَّ لِلَّهِ أَهْلِينَ مِنَ النَّاسِ. قَالُوا يَا رَسُولَ اللَّهِ مَنْ هُمْ؟ قَالَ: هُمْ أَهْلُ الْقُرْآنِ أَهْلُ اللَّهِ وَخَاصَّتُهُ.

Anas bin Malik ﷺ reported: "The Messenger of Allah ﷺ said, "Allah has His own people among mankind." They said: 'O Messenger of Allah, who are they?' He said, "The people of the Qur'an, they are the people of Allah and those who are closest to Him.""

These are the people whom Allah has singled out with His favors. These are the real Awliyaa of Allah. May Allah make us from them!

For the people that live their lives memorizing, learning and implementing the Book of Allah, they will have this great reward in the next life that is mentioned in a Hadith in *Sunan Abi Dawud*:

عَنْ عَبْدِ اللَّهِ بْنِ عَمْرٍو ﷺ، قَالَ: قَالَ رَسُولُ اللَّهِ ﷺ: يُقَالُ لِصَاحِبِ الْقُرْآنِ اقْرَأْ وَارْتَقِ وَرَتِّلْ كَمَا كُنْتَ تُرَتِّلُ فِي الدُّنْيَا فَإِنَّ مَنْزِلَكَ عِنْدَ آخِرِ آيَةٍ تَقْرَؤُهَا.

Abdullah ibn Amr ibn al-'As ﷺ reported: The Messenger of Allah ﷺ said: One who was devoted to the Qur'an will be told to recite, ascend and recite carefully as he recited carefully when he was in the world, for he will reach his destination when he comes to the last verse he recites.

1. Why is it Important to Memorize the Quran?

The raising of levels for the people who held fast to the Quran exists in the life of this world also. We can see in different narrations how Allah raised up the people of the Quran.

Take for example this Hadith from *Sahih Al-Bukhari*:

عَنْ جَابِرِ بْنِ عَبْدِ اللَّهِ ﷺ قَالَ: كَانَ النَّبِيُّ ﷺ يَجْمَعُ بَيْنَ الرَّجُلَيْنِ مِنْ قَتْلَى أُحُدٍ فِي ثَوْبٍ وَاحِدٍ ثُمَّ يَقُولُ: أَيُّهُمْ أَكْثَرُ أَخْذًا لِلْقُرْآنِ؟ فَإِذَا أُشِيرَ لَهُ إِلَى أَحَدِهِمَا قَدَّمَهُ فِي اللَّحْدِ وَقَالَ: أَنَا شَهِيدٌ عَلَى هَؤُلَاءِ يَوْمَ الْقِيَامَةِ. وَأَمَرَ بِدَفْنِهِمْ فِي دِمَائِهِمْ، وَلَمْ يُغَسَّلُوا وَلَمْ يُصَلَّ عَلَيْهِمْ.

Jabir bin 'Abdullah ﷺ reported: The Prophet ﷺ collected every two martyrs of Uhud in one piece of cloth, then he would ask, "Which of them had more of the Qur'an?" When one of them was pointed out for him, he would put that one first in the grave and say, "I will be a witness for these individuals on the Day of Resurrection." He ordered them to be buried with their blood on their bodies and they were neither washed nor was a funeral prayer offered for them.

This is a huge virtue for the person that memorizes the Quran. The people with the most Quran were favored with being placed in the grave first. This virtue was at the death of an individual, but the next Hadith will show the virtue of memorizing the Quran for a person who is alive. The following Hadith is also from *Sahih Al-Bukhari*:

عَنْ عَمْرِو بْنِ سَلِمَةَ ﷺ، قَالَ قَالَ لِي أَبُو قِلَابَةَ أَلَا تَلْقَاهُ فَتَسْأَلَهُ، قَالَ فَلَقِيتُهُ فَسَأَلْتُهُ فَقَالَ كُنَّا بِمَاءٍ مَمَرَّ النَّاسِ، وَكَانَ يَمُرُّ بِنَا الرُّكْبَانُ فَنَسْأَلُهُمْ مَا لِلنَّاسِ مَا لِلنَّاسِ مَا هَذَا الرَّجُلُ فَيَقُولُونَ يَزْعُمُ أَنَّ اللَّهَ أَوْحَى إِلَيْهِ، أَوْ أَوْحَى اللَّهُ بِكَذَا. فَكُنْتُ أَحْفَظُ ذَلِكَ الْكَلَامَ، وَكَأَنَّمَا يُغْرَى فِي صَدْرِي، وَكَانَتِ الْعَرَبُ تَلَوَّمُ بِإِسْلَامِهِمُ الْفَتْحَ، فَيَقُولُونَ اتْرُكُوهُ وَقَوْمَهُ، فَإِنَّهُ إِنْ ظَهَرَ عَلَيْهِمْ فَهُوَ نَبِيٌّ صَادِقٌ. فَلَمَّا كَانَتْ وَقْعَةُ أَهْلِ الْفَتْحِ بَادَرَ كُلُّ قَوْمٍ بِإِسْلَامِهِمْ، وَبَدَرَ أَبِي قَوْمِي بِإِسْلَامِهِمْ، فَلَمَّا قَدِمَ قَالَ جِئْتُكُمْ وَاللَّهِ مِنْ عِنْدِ النَّبِيِّ ﷺ حَقًّا فَقَالَ: صَلُّوا صَلَاةَ كَذَا فِي حِينِ كَذَا، وَصَلُّوا كَذَا فِي حِينِ كَذَا، فَإِذَا حَضَرَتِ الصَّلَاةُ، فَلْيُؤَذِّنْ أَحَدُكُمْ، وَلْيَؤُمَّكُمْ

1. Why is it Important to Memorize the Quran?

أَكْثَرُكُمْ قُرْآنًا. فَنَظَرُوا فَلَمْ يَكُنْ أَحَدٌ أَكْثَرَ قُرْآنًا مِنِّي، لِمَا كُنْتُ أَتَلَقَّى مِنَ الرُّكْبَانِ، فَقَدَّمُونِي بَيْنَ أَيْدِيهِمْ، وَأَنَا ابْنُ سِتٍّ أَوْ سَبْعِ سِنِينَ وَكَانَتْ عَلَيَّ بُرْدَةٌ، كُنْتُ إِذَا سَجَدْتُ تَقَلَّصَتْ عَنِّي، فَقَالَتِ امْرَأَةٌ مِنَ الْحَيِّ أَلَا تُغَطُّوا عَنَّا اسْتَ قَارِئِكُمْ. فَاشْتَرَوْا فَقَطَعُوا لِي قَمِيصًا، فَمَا فَرِحْتُ بِشَيْءٍ فَرَحِي بِذَلِكَ الْقَمِيصِ.

'Amr ibn Salama ﷺ reported: We were at a place which was a thoroughfare for the people, and the caravans used to pass by us and we would ask them, "What is wrong with the people? What is wrong with the people? Who is that man? They would say, "That man claims that Allah has sent him, that he has been divinely inspired, that Allah has revealed to him such-and-such." I used to memorize that (Divine) Talk, and feel as if it was inculcated in my chest (i.e. mind) And the 'Arabs (other than Quraish) delayed their conversion to Islam till the Conquest (of Mecca). They used to say." "Leave him (i.e. Muhammad) and his people Quraish: if he overpowers them then he is a true Prophet. So, when Mecca was conquered, then every tribe rushed to embrace Islam, and my father hurried to embrace Islam before (the other members of) my tribe. When my father returned (from the Prophet) to his tribe, he said, "By Allah, I have come to you from the Prophet (ﷺ) for sure!" The Prophet ﷺ afterwards said to them, 'Offer such-and-such prayer at such-and-such time, and when the time for the prayer becomes due, then one of you should pronounce the *Adhan* (for the prayer), and let the one amongst you who knows Qur'an most lead the prayer." So, they looked for such a person and found none who knew more Qur'an than I because of the Quran which I used to learn from the caravans. They therefore made me their Imam, and at that time, I was a boy of six or seven years, wearing a *Burda* (i.e. a black square garment) proved to be very short for me, so when I prostrated, the garment would lift up leaving my backside exposed. A lady from the tribe said, "Won't you cover the anus of your reciter for us?" So, they bought (a piece of cloth) and made a shirt for me. I had never been so happy with anything before as I was with that shirt.

Whenever I read this Hadith, I always laugh at the end. Even as I was writing this.

We can see from this Hadith that Amr ibn Salamah ﷺ was

1. Why is it Important to Memorize the Quran?

made the Imam of his people at such a young age because of the Quran that he memorized. That is a huge responsibility for such a young child. He carried out his responsibility with the assistance of Allah. Allah raised this young child with the Quran to be a leader among his people. That is no joke. Anybody that understands Arab tribes and their customs will be amazed that a young boy like that became their Imam in the *Salat*. This Hadith should show you that when it comes to the commands of the Messenger of Allah ﷺ, the people put their emotions and customs to the side in obedience to those commands.

We can see a similar story with Abdullah ibn Abbas ؓ and the elders of Badr. This narration is also in *Sahih Al-Bukhari*:

عَنِ ابْنِ عَبَّاسٍ ؓ، قَالَ كَانَ عُمَرُ يُدْخِلُنِي مَعَ أَشْيَاخِ بَدْرٍ، فَكَأَنَّ بَعْضَهُمْ وَجَدَ فِي نَفْسِهِ فَقَالَ لِمَ تُدْخِلُ هَذَا مَعَنَا وَلَنَا أَبْنَاءٌ مِثْلُهُ فَقَالَ عُمَرُ إِنَّهُ مِنْ حَيْثُ عَلِمْتُمْ. فَدَعَا ذَاتَ يَوْمٍ فَأَدْخَلَهُ مَعَهُمْ فَمَا رُئِيتُ أَنَّهُ دَعَانِي يَوْمَئِذٍ إِلاَّ لِيُرِيَهُمْ. قَالَ مَا تَقُولُونَ فِي قَوْلِ اللَّهِ تَعَالَى ﴿إِذَا جَاءَ نَصْرُ اللَّهِ وَالْفَتْحُ﴾ فَقَالَ بَعْضُهُمْ أُمِرْنَا نَحْمَدُ اللَّهَ وَنَسْتَغْفِرُهُ، إِذَا نُصِرْنَا وَفُتِحَ عَلَيْنَا. وَسَكَتَ بَعْضُهُمْ فَلَمْ يَقُلْ شَيْئًا فَقَالَ لِي أَكَذَاكَ تَقُولُ يَا ابْنَ عَبَّاسٍ فَقُلْتُ لاَ. قَالَ فَمَا تَقُولُ قُلْتُ هُوَ أَجَلُ رَسُولِ اللَّهِ ﷺ أَعْلَمَهُ لَهُ، قَالَ ﴿إِذَا جَاءَ نَصْرُ اللَّهِ وَالْفَتْحُ﴾ وَذَلِكَ عَلَامَةُ أَجَلِكَ ﴿فَسَبِّحْ بِحَمْدِ رَبِّكَ وَاسْتَغْفِرْهُ إِنَّهُ كَانَ تَوَّابًا﴾. فَقَالَ عُمَرُ مَا أَعْلَمُ مِنْهَا إِلاَّ مَا تَقُولُ.

Ibn `Abbas ؓ reported: `Umar used to make me sit with the elderly men who had fought in the Battle of Badr. Some of them did not like that and said to `Umar, "Why do you bring in this boy to sit with us while we have sons his age?" `Umar replied, "Because of what you know of his position (i.e. his religious knowledge.)" One day `Umar called me and made me sit in the gathering of those people; and I think that he called me just to show them (my religious knowledge). `Umar then asked them, "What do you say about the interpretation of the Statement of Allah: '*When comes Help of Allah (to you O, Muhammad against your enemies) and the conquest (of Mecca).*' *(110:1)* Some of them said, "We are ordered to praise Allah and ask for His forgiveness when Allah's Help and the conquest (of Mecca) comes to us." Some others kept quiet and did not say anything. On that, 'Umar asked me, "Do you say the same, O Ibn 'Abbas?" I replied, "No." He said, 'What do you say then?" I replied, "That is the sign of the death of Allah's Messenger (ﷺ) which Allah informed him of. Allah said, '(O Muhammad) When comes the Help of Allah (to you against your enemies) and the conquest (of Mecca),' which is the sign of your death, 'You should celebrate the praises of your Lord and ask for His Forgiveness, and He is the One Who accepts the repentance and forgives.' (110:1,3) On that 'Umar said, "I do not know anything regarding the interpretation if this *Surah* other than what you have said."

Allah raised Ibn Abbas ﷺ with the knowledge of the Quran. If we took the Quran in the manner that Allah commanded Yahya to take the Book He revealed, we will be successful too, and Allah will raise us the way He raised those before us. Allah said in the Quran:

﴿يَٰيَحْيَىٰ خُذِ ٱلْكِتَٰبَ بِقُوَّةٍ ۖ وَءَاتَيْنَٰهُ ٱلْحُكْمَ صَبِيًّا﴾

"O Yahya! Hold firmly to the Scriptures." And We granted him wisdom while he was still a child. [19:12]

According to Imam At-Tabri, the meaning of the *Ayah* is for Yahya to take the Book with seriousness. Do not take it as a joke. The Book is meant to be read, learned and implemented. The Book is not entertainment. Imam At-Tabri also mentioned that the wisdom that was given to Yahya at a young age was the understanding of the Book. Again, we see how Allah raised up the righteous youth with the Revelation.

It is time that we wake up as Muslims and recognize why we are in the state we are in. We are in this sad state because we have strayed away from Allah's Book. We have strayed away from the Sunnah of Allah's Final Messenger ﷺ. If we want to return to glory, we need to take the path of the people before us that were successful. The people I am referring to are our *Salaf* or Pious Predecessors. This was made clear as day in a statement from Imam Malik ibn Anas:

لا يصلح آخر هذه الأمة إلا بما صلح به أولها

1. Why is it Important to Memorize the Quran?

> The rectification of the latter part of this Ummah can only occur with that which rectified the first part of this Ummah.

What made them successful was following the Quran and the Sunnah the way it was taught to them by the Messenger of Allah ﷺ. They were successful by memorizing the Book of Allah, learning it and acting on it. That is the only way we can return to glory. We will never be a strong nation again going out to the streets protesting with the kuffaar and women. We will never be a strong nation again by getting involved in politics. We will never be a strong nation again by seeking validation from the enemies of Allah. We have the criteria for success, and that criterion is in the Quran and the Sunnah. There is no other way.

Imam Ash-Shaafi' said in a poem of his:

إلّا الحَديثَ وَعِلمَ الفِقهِ في الدينِ   كُلُّ العُلومِ سِوى القُرآنِ مَشغَلَةٌ
وَمــا سِــوى ذاكَ وَسـواسُ الشَــياطينِ   العِلمُ ما كانَ فيهِ قالَ حَدَّثَنا

Every science other than the Quran is a distraction except Al-Hadith and the science of *Fiqh* in this *Deen*. Knowledge is comprised of "it was narrated to us," and anything else is from the whisperings of the devils.

Beneficial knowledge is knowledge that assists you in the understanding of the Quran and the Sunnah. Everything else is a distraction. May Allah keep us busy with that which brings us benefit in this life and the next!

CHAPTER 2:
Habits One Needs to Develop to Memorize the Quran

As I stated previously, almost every Muslim will say that he has a goal to memorize the Quran. Some people are serious and most are not. The one thing that will determine who will be successful in the end, after the *tawfeeq* of Allah of course, is who is prepared to make the sacrifices and lifestyle changes necessary to be successful in his memorization journey.

In this chapter, I will focus on those lifestyle changes that need to happen for the goal to become a reality *insha'Allah.* This chapter is not going to cover every change that needs to be covered, but it will give each person an idea of the changes that he needs to make in his own life.

In my previous book, *The Believer's Handbook for Seeking Knowledge,* I discussed the characteristics that one needs to be successful in his studies. Those characteristics still apply here. In fact, those characteristics are tied into the habits that match each characteristic, but you will have to make that connection.

HABIT 1

The first habit you have to develop is a reading program for the Quran. Even before you begin memorizing the Quran, you have to develop a plan for every morning for the amount Quran that you are going to read that day. It does not matter if you are reading one *Juz* or ten. Whatever you plan to read that day, do it and stick to it.

If you do not get in the habit of reading the Quran every day consistently, you will find it very difficult to continue memorizing on a daily basis. It is a lot easier to sit down and read the Quran than it is to memorize it.

The type of reading program you develop will be based on what you have already memorized from the Quran. If you have not memorized *Juz* Amma, you will begin by reading the last three *Juz* from the Quran. Read *Juz* 28 one day, *Juz* 29 the next day, and *Juz* 30 the final day. Once you complete the three days, repeat. You will repeat these three over and over until you are close to finishing the memorization of them. Once you finish memorizing *Juz* 28, add another *Juz* for each day.

Your schedule will then become reading *Juz* 25 and *Juz* 26 on the first day, *Juz* 27 and *Juz* 28 on the second day, and *Juz* 29 and *Juz* 30 on the last day. When you are about the complete the memorization of these *Juz*, add another day to make it two *Juz* a day for four days instead of just three. Keep adding like this until you finish the entire Quran.

You want to work up to the point of being able to read five *Juz* every day for six days. At this point, you will read the Quran five times every month and 60 times a year.

Once you get comfortable with your morning reading, and you have formulated a habit, you must add a time for reading before you go to bed. The reading that you will do before you go to bed will be the *Juz* that you are working on at that time. You do not have to read an entire *Juz*; you can read half of a *Juz* if you do not have the time. The important thing is that you read what you are memorizing every evening before bed. You will notice how much your memory improves with this method.

To develop this reading habit, you will need to discipline yourself every day. There are going to be so many days that you will try to convince yourself to take a day off. Do not listen to yourself. Pick up the *Mus'haf* and get to work. The first two weeks will be a bit difficult, but

2. Habits One Needs to Develop to Memorize the Quran

you will find that the reading will get easier and easier. After a month of self-discipline, you will find that once you finish reading, you will have so much energy and desire to read more. At this point, you have to discipline yourself to not do too much too soon. Stick with your plan.

HABIT 2

You have to fix your sleep schedule. Your goal is to wake up 30 minutes to an hour before Fajr, so you can get your day started early without distractions. Most people are accustomed to sleeping to the last minute, but you cannot afford to waste those precious minutes being lazy and procrastinating. Beginning your day by hitting the snooze button until the last minute is already starting your day off with failure. You have to win the battle over yourself from the beginning of the day.

The most ideal time to wake up, especially in the winter time, is two hours before Fajr. You need to get up, drink some water, make wudhu, and get started with the things you need to get done. This time in the last third of the night is a time of dua and a time for the remembrance of Allah. There is no better remembrance of Allah than with His Book. This is the time of day that your mind will be the clearest, especially if you got a good night's sleep.

Obviously, to wake up early, you need to go to bed early. To make going to bed early a habit, you have to avoid all the pitfalls that people fall into. Those pitfalls include talking too much after the Isha prayer, using your phone or laptop before sleeping, drinking caffeinated beverages late in the afternoon, worrying about things, drinking too much water, etc. Whatever causes you to find difficulty sleeping early, get rid of it.

Take the Sunnah of the Messenger of Allah ﷺ as the best example for your sleeping schedule:

عن أبي برزة ﷺ أن رسول الله ﷺ كان يكره النوم قبل العشاء والحديث بعدها.

2. Habits One Needs to Develop to Memorize the Quran

Abu Barzah ؓ said, "The Messenger of Allah ﷺ disliked going to bed before the 'Isha' (night) prayer and indulging in conversation after it."

This Hadith, which is in *Al-Bukhari* and *Muslim,* clearly shows the Prophet's ﷺ habit before going to sleep. He disliked sleeping before Isha because it would cause him to remain awake for a large portion of the night, and he disliked conversation after Isha because it would lead to him falling asleep later and maybe not waking up for the night prayer. The Prophet's ﷺ concern was to have energy for the prayer at night. That meant getting sufficient sleep after Isha. It is difficult to wake up in the last third of the night to pray after you sat up staring at a phone screen until midnight. Most people that enjoy entertainment late into the night will miss out on all the benefits in the early part of the morning.

Your success will be in what you get done in the early part of the morning, and anything that keeps you from having energy in the early hours of the morning is going to bring you failure, disappointment and regret.

The Prophet ﷺ stated in the following Hadith from *Sunan At-Tirmidhi*:

عـن صخـر بن وداعـة الغامـدي الصحـابي ؓ أن رسـول الله ﷺ قـال: اللهـم بـارك لأمتـي في بكورهـا. وكان إذا بعـث سـرية أو جيشـاً بعثـهم مـن أول النهـار. وكان صخـر تاجـراً فكان يبعـث تجارتـه أول النهـار، فـأثري وكثر مـاله.

Sakhr bin Wada'ah Al-Ghamidi ؓ reported: The Messenger of Allah ﷺ said, "O Allah! Bless my people in the early part of the morning. Whenever he dispatched a detachment or an army-unit, he would dispatch it at the beginning of the day (soon after dawn). The narrator, Sakhr (ؓ) was a merchant, and he used to send off his merchandise at the beginning of the day. His trade flourished and he made a good fortune.

For you to be a part of this dua of the Prophet ﷺ, you have to get busy in the early morning. Don't allow laziness, procrastination and love for entertainment keep you from benefitting from this time of day. Successful people do not sleep the day away. Successful people get their day started while the losers of the world continue to snore.

HABIT 3

If your diet is in disarray, you will have to fix it. For most people in the West, this is the most difficult habit to fix. Fast food, soft drinks and lattes have become the norm of a dumbed down populace. You cannot follow the path of the losers if you want to be successful.

Eating healthy is essential for anybody that wants to be successful in any activity that requires physical or mental exertion. It is difficult to have energy and mental clarity needed for the task at hand when you are malnourished from the day before with potato chips, ice cream and Dr. Pepper. If you want energy and mental clarity, you will have to change your food and drink choices to make sure you establish a diet that provides the nutrients you need for what you have to do.

For you to change your diet, you have to first change your mindset. You have to come to terms with what is more important to you: eating for desire or eating for energy. The answer you choose from these two choices will dictate your food choices. Obviously, you have to develop the mindset of eating for energy and health over eating out of desire. However, eating for health is not sufficient because there is an abundance of healthy foods that are known to be bad for memory. For example, eating a lot of citrus fruits has been known among the Ulema of the past to weaken the memory. Also eating a lot of bitter foods can also weaken the memory. Drinking a lot of coffee has been known to weaken the memory over time. This last example is one people do not like a lot, especially people on Twitter.

The issue of food is two-fold. There is the issue of the amount of food one consumes, and there is the issue of the type of foods one

2. Habits One Needs to Develop to Memorize the Quran

takes in. The amount of food is the most important issue. If a person overeats with healthy food, he will destroy his health the same as if he ate too much unhealthy food. In fact, the person who eats little food that is not fully nutritious is better than the person who overeats with a lot of food that is nutritious.

Imam Ash-Shaafi' considered this from the things that destroy a person in the following poem attributed to him:

ثَلَاثٌ هُنَّ مُهلِكَةُ الأَنَامِ   وَداعِيَةُ الصَّحيحِ إِلى السِّقامِ

دَوامُ مُدامَةٍ وَدَوامُ وَطءٍ   وَإِدخالُ الطَّعامِ عَلى الطَّعامِ

Three things destroy mankind, and call a healthy person to a state of sickness. Constantly drinking alcohol, constantly having sexual intercourse, and placing food on top of food.

Drinking alcohol is prohibited, so that should not even be an issue. However, a major issue among Muslims nowadays is smoking weed. There have been some fools who decided that because marijuana grows from the earth, and it is now used for medicinal purposes that it is *halal*. What stupidity! This is nothing more than a person of desires taking knowledge from shaytan in order to justify following his desires.

Marijuana makes a person stupid. Take a person who smokes marijuana every day and put him in a class to learn Arabic and see what he can do. He will more than likely be the slowest person in the class. In fact, I have yet to see a person who smokes marijuana every day be consistent in any class. That is because another side of effect of this drug is that it makes a person lazy and sluggish. If you want to see a loser that has no goals, no passion for anything and no determination to do anything, just look at a person that smokes weed every day.

Marijuana also slows down the function of the mind, which makes memorization ten times harder for the person who smokes weed than the one who does not. So, I would not be expecting a weed smoking scholar any time soon. I am surprised if I see a weed smoker in America that can even recite *Surah Al-Fatihah*.

The next thing Imam Ash-Shaafi' mentioned was constantly

2. Habits One Needs to Develop to Memorize the Quran

engaging in sexual intercourse. Too much of anything is not good, and this is no exception. Too much sexual intercourse weakens the body. With any type of exertion, the body needs a recovery period. If you keep pushing your body without recovery, you will face the consequences later in life. This is why we see elite athletes refraining from all forms of sexual activity in the weeks leading up to a competition. They will tell you that the sexual activity reduces their strength, and that is the cause for their abstaining.

Moreover, a man should have goals that he is working towards and responsibilities that he is taking care of. That means that he is not going to have the energy to exert himself in this act every single day. The person that you see overindulging in this act is the lazy person that sleeps all day, has no responsibilities and does not work. As Muslims, we take the middle course in everything we do, and that includes this act. Ice cream tastes better when you do not eat it so much. If you eat ice cream every day, it does not taste so good. The same thing with the enjoyment one gets out of sexual intercourse. By taking two days off or more if needed and allowing your body to repair, you get more enjoyment out of the act.

The third thing that Imam Ash-Shaafi' mentioned is putting food on food. This means that a person eats another meal before the previous one is digested. This completely destroys the body over time. Once you eat, you should allow the digestive process to work without any interruption from food or drink.

You should stop drinking liquids close to one hour before you eat, and you should not resume drinking liquids until an hour has passed since you last consumed food. This is to keep the digestive juices in the stomach from becoming watered down which will cause the digestive system to function at a slower rate. Never drink with your meals if you can avoid it.

You should also not eat again until you feel that you are actually hungry and the previous food you ate is completely digested. This means that you will be eating fewer meals with smaller amounts of food. The ideal situation is for a person to consume two meals a day. I brought

2. Habits One Needs to Develop to Memorize the Quran

the statement by Sahl At-Tusturi regarding this issue in my book *The Believer's Handbook for Seeking Knowledge*, so you can refer back to the chapter in that book.

HABIT 4

The next habit is going to be difficult for a lot of people. This is the habit of doing away with a lot of the foolish things we waste our time with. As you get further along in your memorization journey, you will see how much time is required each day to read, memorize, and revise. You will also realize that you will not be able to make time for these actions without doing away with a lot of those time-wasting actions you are accustomed to doing.

If you are accustomed to spending countless hours on social media going back-and-forth with people that have all the free time in the world, you will not accomplish much in this life. To be successful in any endeavor, you have to become a stranger to the people. You have to dedicate the majority of your free time to completing the memorization of the Quran, which means you will not have a lot of time left over for the people. I am not telling you to refrain completely from sitting with the people, but I am saying fulfill your obligations towards your goal first, and give the people whatever is left over from your time.

Other people might waste their time watching TV. Other people might waste their time going out all the time. Whatever your vice might be, begin removing it from your life and replacing it with actions that bring you closer to achieving your goal of memorizing the Quran.

HABIT 5

The next thing is a person should get in the habit of listening to the Quran regularly. If you are a person that listens to music, you should know that the Quran and music will never come together in one heart. The Quran calls a person to Eman, and music calls a person to hypocrisy.

2. Habits One Needs to Develop to Memorize the Quran

You cannot combine between love for Eman and love for hypocrisy in one heart. If music is going in, Quran is going out. Furthermore, music is haram. Allah said in the Quran:

﴿وَمِنَ ٱلنَّاسِ مَن يَشْتَرِى لَهْوَ ٱلْحَدِيثِ لِيُضِلَّ عَن سَبِيلِ ٱللَّهِ بِغَيْرِ عِلْمٍ وَيَتَّخِذَهَا هُزُوًا أُوْلَٰٓئِكَ لَهُمْ عَذَابٌ مُّهِينٌ﴾

But there are some who employ foolish speech only to lead others away from Allah's Way without any knowledge and to make a mockery of it. They will suffer a humiliating punishment. [31:6]

Ibn Kathir mentioned about this *Ayah* from *Surah Luqman*:

عطف بذكر حال الأشقياء الذين أعرضوا عن الانتفاع بسماع كلام الله ، وأقبلوا على استماع المزامير والغناء بالألحان وآلات الطرب ، كما قال ابن مسعود في قوله تعالى : (ومن الناس من يشتري لهو الحديث) قال : هو - والله - الغناء .

Allah connected the mentioning of the people of the hellfire that turned their backs on listening to the Speech of Allah with their turning towards listening to flutes, singing with rhythm and musical instruments. Ibn Masood ؓ said about the statement of Allah "From among the people are those that sell foolish speech": It is, I swear by Allah, referring to music.

Imam Ash-Sha'bi has a beautiful statement in regard to music in which he said:

إن الغناء ينبت النفاق في القلب كما ينبت الماء الزرع، وإن الذكر ينبت الإيمان في القلب كما ينبت الماء الزرع.

Verily, music causes the growth of hypocrisy in the heart like water causes the plants to grow, and the remembrance of Allah causes Eman to grow in the heart like water causes the plants to grow.

Imam Ibn Al-Qayyim also mentioned about this issue:

2. Habits One Needs to Develop to Memorize the Quran

فاعلم أن للغناء خواص. لها تأثير في صبغ القلب بالنفاق ونباته فيه كنبات الزرع بالماء، فمن خواصه: أنه يلهي القلب ويصده عن فهم القرآن وتدبره والعمل بما فيه، فإن القرآن والغناء لا يجتمعان في القلب أبدا لما بينهما من التضاد، فإن القرآن ينهى عن اتباع الهوى ويأمر بالعفة ومجانبة شهوات النفوس وأسباب الغي، وينهى عن اتباع خطوات الشيطان، والغناء يأمر بضد ذلك كله

> Know that music has bad effects that are not found in other sins. Music has the effect of dyeing the heart with hypocrisy and causing hypocrisy to grow in the heart like water causes the plants to grow. From its bad effects are that it distracts the heart and blocks it from understanding and pondering the Quran and acting upon what is in the Quran. For verily, the Quran and music will never gather together in the heart due to the contradiction that exists between the two. The Quran prohibits the following of desires, commands people to show decency, it commands people to refrain from the desires of the self and the means of deviation, and it prohibits people from following in the footsteps of shaytan. Music commands people with the opposite of all that was mentioned.

There remains no doubt that music causes the total corruption of the heart. Music also opens up the heart to others sins that will cause the destruction of the one that chooses to listen to music over the Quran. This is the fitnah of these Last Days, especially with these liberal YouTube shaykhs who change the Deen to assimilate the Muslims into the culture of the kuffaar. We were warned to beware of these deviants in the Last Days by the Messenger of Allah ﷺ in a Hadith in *Sahih Al-Bukhari*:

عن أبي عامر أو أبي مالك الأشعري ﷺ قال: سمعت النبي ﷺ يقول: لَيَكُونَنَّ مِنْ أُمَّتِي أَقْوَامٌ يَسْتَحِلُّونَ الْحِرَ وَالْحَرِيرَ وَالْخَمْرَ وَالْمَعَازِفَ، وَلَيَنْزِلَنَّ أَقْوَامٌ إِلَى جَنْبِ عَلَمٍ يَرُوحُ عَلَيْهِمْ بِسَارِحَةٍ لَهُمْ، يَأْتِيهِمْ يَعْنِي الْفَقِيرَ لِحَاجَةٍ فَيَقُولُوا ارْجِعْ إِلَيْنَا غَدًا. فَيُبَيِّتُهُمُ اللَّهُ وَيَضَعُ الْعَلَمَ، وَيَمْسَخُ آخَرِينَ قِرَدَةً وَخَنَازِيرَ إِلَى يَوْمِ الْقِيَامَةِ.

2. Habits One Needs to Develop to Memorize the Quran

Abu 'Amir or Abu Malik Al-Ash'ari ﷺ reported: He heard the Prophet ﷺ saying, "From among my Ummah there will be some people who will consider illegal sexual intercourse, the wearing of silk, the drinking of alcoholic drinks and the use of musical instruments, as lawful. And there will be some people who will stay near the side of a mountain and in the evening their shepherd will come to them with their sheep and ask them for something, but they will say to him, 'Return to us tomorrow.' Allah will destroy them during the night and will let the mountain fall on them, and He will transform the rest of them into monkeys and pigs and they will remain so till the Day of Resurrection."

The Prophet ﷺ mentioned first the making of fornication as lawful. We see this nowadays with Muslims in the West and the unlawful marriages they get involved in. A person will give a brother a fatwa telling him that he can bypass the father as the Wali because the father does not agree to the marriage. The brother takes this corrupt fatwa and carries it out. His marriage is then invalid. We also see this with the midnight marriages and Walmart bathroom marriages that people do with the sole purpose of seeking enjoyment with the girl and then tossing her to the side once he is finished. There is no difference between these marriages and what the raafidis do. There is no difference between these marriages and people picking up prostitutes. May Allah protect us from falling into this corrupt deviant behavior.

The Prophet ﷺ then mentioned the wearing of silk. He is speaking about the wearing of silk for men. We have seen more than that nowadays. We see Muslims making earrings, necklaces and bracelets permissible for men to wear. Since I have been back in America, I have seen more Muslims wearing necklaces and earrings than I have ever seen. I was shocked when I came back.

The Prophet ﷺ mentioned alcoholic drinks. We see this among the Muslims a lot now. In fact, a lot of the liquor stores are owned by so-called Muslims. Weed has been made halal among the Muslims that love to follow their desires as I already mentioned previously.

The final thing the Prophet ﷺ mentioned was that these

corrupt ruwaibidah will make musical instruments *halal.* We have seen this more than we have seen any of the other things the Prophet ﷺ mentioned. These things become halal when people put their desires at the forefront. They are not looking for the truth; they are looking to satiate their corrupt appetites. Allah said about these people in the Quran:

﴿أَفَرَءَيْتَ مَنِ ٱتَّخَذَ إِلَٰهَهُۥ هَوَىٰهُ وَأَضَلَّهُ ٱللَّهُ عَلَىٰ عِلْمٍ وَخَتَمَ عَلَىٰ سَمْعِهِۦ وَقَلْبِهِۦ وَجَعَلَ عَلَىٰ بَصَرِهِۦ غِشَٰوَةً فَمَن يَهْدِيهِ مِنۢ بَعْدِ ٱللَّهِ أَفَلَا تَذَكَّرُونَ﴾

Have you seen those who have taken their own desires as their god? And so, Allah left them to stray knowingly, sealed their hearing and hearts, and placed a cover on their sight. Who then can guide them after Allah? Will you all not then be mindful? [45:23]

Allah also mentioned what happens to the people that follow those that follow their desires in the following *Ayah*:

﴿وَإِن تُطِعْ أَكْثَرَ مَن فِى ٱلْأَرْضِ يُضِلُّوكَ عَن سَبِيلِ ٱللَّهِ إِن يَتَّبِعُونَ إِلَّا ٱلظَّنَّ وَإِنْ هُمْ إِلَّا يَخْرُصُونَ﴾

If you were to obey most of those on earth, they would lead you away from Allah's Way. They follow nothing but false assumptions and do nothing but lie. [6:116]

The people of desires cause nothing but corruption and misguidance, and they should never be listened to nor obeyed.

However, not everybody is afflicted with the fitnah of music. Some people just waste their time listening to useless podcasts or other nonsense to be found on YouTube. Whatever the case is with a person, he should focus on switching out the habit of listening to other than the Quran to listening to the Quran, especially if he wants to memorize it.

2. Habits One Needs to Develop to Memorize the Quran

One of the most important benefits of listening to the Quran is that it aids in the memorization. Listening to the Quran constantly causes the Speech of Allah to get stored in the long-term memory of a person. When this happens, memorizing the Quran becomes so much easier. I think most adults that grew up around music can even remember lyrics to songs they heard as a child or teenager. Sometimes lyrics will pop in my head from songs that I heard 30 years ago. That is because I heard the song so much that it was stored in the long-term memory, so it is not easily forgotten. You now must do that with the Quran.

HABIT 6

One of the best actions to make a habit out of for the person memorizing the Quran is to stand up at night in prayer. I do not know of a better action to assist a person in his memorization journey than this action. Standing up at night in prayer has so many benefits for the Student of Knowledge, and here are a few:

- Praying at night assists with revision of the Quran;
- Praying at night is a means to have a lot of sins forgiven;
- The *dua* in the last third of the night is answered;
- Praying at night accustoms the person to using the Quran in prayer;
- The night prayer was always a custom of the Prophet ﷺ.

There are many more benefits, but these are a few. For a person who is not an Imam in a Masjid, the night prayer gives him the practice of reciting in the *Salat* from memory. This is good practice for a person that might end up as an Imam in a Masjid.

If you are a person not accustomed to praying at night, winter is the best time to get in this habit. The nights are long and the days are shorter. You can get up at the same time you were praying Fajr in the summer and pray for 30–45 minutes easily.

You should also not think that you have to go overboard and

2. Habits One Needs to Develop to Memorize the Quran

pray for three hours every night. You can begin with seven *rakahs*, which include four normal *rakahs* and three *rakahs* of *Witr*. You can revise one *Surah* in each *rakah*. The following might be a good example:

- 1st *Rakah*: *Surah Al-Dhaariyaat*;
- 2nd *Rakah*: *Surah At-Tur*;
- 3rd *Rakah*: *Surah An-Najm*;
- 4th *Rakah*: *Surah Al-Qamr*;
- Then you pray *Witr*.

Depending on how long you spend in *Ruku'* and *Sujood*, this could last from 30 minutes to one hour. If you have little time, pray a bit faster, and if you have more time, prayer for longer. The important thing is to get something done even if it is a little and to be consistent with what you do.

The Prophet ﷺ mentioned consistency in the night prayer in the following Hadith from *Al-Bukhari* and *Muslim*:

عَنْ عَبْدِ اللهِ بْنِ عَمْرِو بْنِ الْعَاصِ ﷺ قَالَ: قَالَ لِي رَسُولُ اللهِ ﷺ: يَا عَبْدَ اللهِ، لَا تَكُنْ مِثْلَ فُلَانٍ، كَانَ يَقُومُ اللَّيْلَ فَتَرَكَ قِيَامَ اللَّيْلِ.

'Abdullah bin 'Amr bin Al-'as ﷺ reported: Messenger of Allah ﷺ said to me, "O 'Abdullah! Do not be like so-and-so; he used to get up at night for optional prayer but abandoned it later.

The Prophet ﷺ was advising Abdullah ibn Amr ﷺ to be consistent in his night prayer. Even if it is a little. Allah loves actions that are done consistently, even if they are few. The following Hadith from *Al-Bukhari* and *Muslim* express this meaning:

عَنْ عَائِشَةَ ﷺ أَنَّهَا قَالَتْ سُئِلَ النَّبِيُّ ﷺ أَيُّ الْأَعْمَالِ أَحَبُّ إِلَى اللهِ قَالَ: أَدْوَمُهَا وَإِنْ قَلَّ. وَقَالَ: اكْلَفُوا مِنَ الْأَعْمَالِ مَا تُطِيقُونَ.

'Aisha ﷺ reported: The Prophet ﷺ was asked, "What deeds are loved most by Allah?" He said, "The most regular constant deeds even though they may be few." He added, 'Don't take upon yourselves, except the deeds which are within your ability."

Try your best to get up and get something done. Just make sure you remain consistent in what you do.

HABIT 7

You must also start some type of exercise and stretching program. Memorizing the Quran involves a lot of sitting in one place for prolonged periods of time. This can cause weakness and stiffness in the body over time. To combat these effects, it is good to exercise a little and to stretch every day.

Whatever form of exercise you choose is up to you. You can do calisthenics, go out and play a little basketball, swim, lift weights, jump rope, run, etc. The important thing is to keep exercising to a limit. You do not want to turn exercise into the focus. If you exercise too much, you will not have the energy to memorize every day. Exercise should be done at least three to four times per week. Stretching should be done every day to keep the blood flowing to all parts of the body and to combat stiffness.

Stretching every day will also assist you in your ability to sit longer while you are memorizing. It is very difficult to memorize when your body starts to tighten up after sitting for half an hour.

HABIT 8

You have to get in the habit of reading the Quran from cover to cover. Even when you are memorizing, you have to stop for small periods of time and just read the Quran over and over. Ramadan will always be dedicated to that, but you should also schedule this into other months of the year.

On average, you should try to read the Quran 12 times per year. You can split it up however you want. I prefer to start off the first ten days of every month reading the entire *Mus'haf*, and for the rest of the month, I will focus on what I am memorizing. You can also just take a

2. Habits One Needs to Develop to Memorize the Quran

Juz a day that you read from the *Mus'haf*, and you will end up finishing the entire Quran 12 times. However you decide to complete the task is up to you, but the important thing is to get it done.

As you progress more and more in your memorization, you will want to increase the number of times per year that you read the entire *Mus'haf*. The *Salaf* were known to have read the Quran one thousand times and more. Nowadays, you might experience difficulty finding a Student of Knowledge that has read the entire Quran 100 times.

CHAPTER 3:
Actions Which Will Assist You During Your Memorization

The purpose of this chapter is to detail actions one can do outside of the actual memorization plan to make memorizing the Quran much easier. The actions here involve reading, writing and listening. Like any new science one wishes to master, a person must completely engross himself in that science. Being that our focus here is memorizing the Quran, these extra actions will aid in that engrossing of ourselves in this matter.

ACTION 1: LEARN THE ARABIC LANGUAGE

I would hope this would be a given. One should learn the Arabic language because it is an obligation upon every Muslim to know enough Arabic to understand the commands and prohibitions in the Quran and the Sunnah. There is no excuse for a person to be careless with the language.

Imam Ash-Shaafi' mentioned the following in regards to the ruling on learning the Arabic language in his book *Ar-Risalah*:

فعلى كل مسلم أن يتعلم من لسان العرب ما بلغه جهده، حتى يَشْهَد به أنْ لا إله إلا الله، وأنَّ محمدا عبده ورسوله ﷺ ويتلوَ به كتابَ الله، وينطق بالذكر فيما افتُرِض عليه من التكبير، وأمر به من التسبيح، والتشهد، وغيرِ ذلك.

3. Actions Which Will Assist You During Your Memorization

It is binding upon every Muslim to learn the Arabic language to the best of his capabilities, so he can bear witness that none has the right to be worshipped except Allah and Muhammad ﷺ is His servant and Messenger, and he can recite the book of Allah, say the different adhkaar that have been made obligatory upon him from the takbeer, the tasbeeh, the tasha'hud, and other forms of adhkaar.

How can a Muslim go his entire life on this earth and never exert any effort to understand the speech of Allah? That is insane! Do people actually think that reading English translations is sufficient for them? We need to wake the Muslims up out of the coma we find this Ummah in. It is from carelessness, neglect and heedlessness that one does not even attempt to learn the Arabic language. It could also be from arrogance depending on the person. Either way, the punishment for either one is too great if one dies in that state. May Allah protect us!

Allah mentioned the heedless throughout the Quran in a manner that is deserving. Allah said:

﴿وَٱصْبِرْ نَفْسَكَ مَعَ ٱلَّذِينَ يَدْعُونَ رَبَّهُم بِٱلْغَدَوٰةِ وَٱلْعَشِيِّ يُرِيدُونَ وَجْهَهُۥ ۖ وَلَا تَعْدُ عَيْنَاكَ عَنْهُمْ تُرِيدُ زِينَةَ ٱلْحَيَوٰةِ ٱلدُّنْيَا ۖ وَلَا تُطِعْ مَنْ أَغْفَلْنَا قَلْبَهُۥ عَن ذِكْرِنَا وَٱتَّبَعَ هَوَىٰهُ وَكَانَ أَمْرُهُۥ فُرُطًا﴾

And patiently stick with those who call upon their Lord morning and evening, seeking His pleasure. Do not let your eyes look beyond them, desiring the luxuries of this worldly life. And do not obey those whose hearts We have made heedless of Our remembrance, who follow only their desires and whose state is total loss. [18:28]

The Prophet ﷺ was commanded to remain patient with the believers and to avoid sitting with the heedless people. Those are the people that have no concern with the *Deen*. The heedless people are the people of desires that will exert 100% effort to get the dunya, but they will not even exert a 10% effort to get the next life. They are not concerned with memorizing the Quran, studying the Arabic language or learning their *Deen*. Their concern is to pray five times a day and fast Ramadan. The rest of their lives is spent on actions which have no benefit in the *Deen*.

Allah also said about the heedless people:

﴿وَلَقَدْ ذَرَأْنَا لِجَهَنَّمَ كَثِيرًا مِّنَ ٱلْجِنِّ وَٱلْإِنسِ ۖ لَهُمْ قُلُوبٌ لَّا يَفْقَهُونَ بِهَا وَلَهُمْ أَعْيُنٌ لَّا يُبْصِرُونَ بِهَا وَلَهُمْ ءَاذَانٌ لَّا يَسْمَعُونَ بِهَآ ۚ أُوْلَـٰٓئِكَ كَٱلْأَنْعَـٰمِ بَلْ هُمْ أَضَلُّ ۚ أُوْلَـٰٓئِكَ هُمُ ٱلْغَـٰفِلُونَ﴾

Indeed, We have created many jinn and humans for Hell. They have hearts they do not understand with, eyes they do not see with, and ears they do not hear with. They are like livestock. In fact, they are even less guided! Such people are completely heedless. [7:179]

All the faculties that Allah has given us: sight, hearing and a heart to perceive and understand, and the heedless people never use these faculties in the obedience to Allah. They either use them for the disobedience of Allah or to get the life of this world. Allah said in the Quran:

﴿وَٱللَّهُ أَخْرَجَكُم مِّنۢ بُطُونِ أُمَّهَـٰتِكُمْ لَا تَعْلَمُونَ شَيْـًٔا وَجَعَلَ لَكُمُ ٱلسَّمْعَ وَٱلْأَبْصَـٰرَ وَٱلْأَفْـِٔدَةَ ۙ لَعَلَّكُمْ تَشْكُرُونَ﴾

And Allah brought you out of the wombs of your mothers while you knew nothing, and gave you hearing, sight, and intellect so perhaps you would be thankful. [16:78]

Show gratitude to Allah by learning His *Deen* and obeying Him with the knowledge that He has gifted you. The way you show your gratitude is through your obedience to Him. How can you be considered grateful to the One you openly disobey without any concern?

Not being concerned with learning the Arabic language is

3. Actions Which Will Assist You During Your Memorization

turning away from the Revelation. This is a form of turning your back on what Allah sent down. How can you live your life without being concerned that you do not understand the speech of Allah? This is a punishment in the *dunya*. Allah said in the Quran:

﴿ سَأَصْرِفُ عَنْ ءَايَـٰتِىَ ٱلَّذِينَ يَتَكَبَّرُونَ فِى ٱلْأَرْضِ بِغَيْرِ ٱلْحَقِّ وَإِن يَرَوْاْ كُلَّ ءَايَةٍ لَّا يُؤْمِنُواْ بِهَا وَإِن يَرَوْاْ سَبِيلَ ٱلرُّشْدِ لَا يَتَّخِذُوهُ سَبِيلًا وَإِن يَرَوْاْ سَبِيلَ ٱلْغَىِّ يَتَّخِذُوهُ سَبِيلًا ۚ ذَٰلِكَ بِأَنَّهُمْ كَذَّبُواْ بِـَٔايَـٰتِنَا وَكَانُواْ عَنْهَا غَـٰفِلِينَ ﴾

I will turn away from My signs those who act unjustly with arrogance in the land. And even if they were to see every sign, they still would not believe in them. If they see the Right Path, they will not take it. But if they see the path of deviance, they will follow it. This is because they denied Our signs and were heedless of them. [7:146]

Arrogance and heedlessness are the causes for a person to neglect his responsibility to learn the Arabic language. What punishment in this *dunya* is greater than Allah not allowing you to understand His speech and the speech of His Messenger? Is there anything more foolish than a person that claims to follow the Quran and the Sunnah, but he exerts zero effort to learn the Arabic language to understand them? How can you consider yourself a follower of something that you do not seek to understand? That is a joke. May Allah guide us all!

As far as how the Arabic language can help you with your memorization of the Quran, it is simple: It is much easier to memorize and retain something you actually understand than something which you do not understand.

When I began studying Arabic, I found a lot of difficulty memorizing the Quran. That was because I was memorizing a lot of foreign words on a page, and I had no idea what was going on. I might understand a word or two, but that was not enough to understand what was being said on the page I was memorizing.

As I began to understand more and more of the Arabic language, my memory became stronger and stronger. Memorization is always going to be difficult. It is something the vast majority of people do not want to do. However, we can lessen the burden on ourselves by actually understanding what we are memorizing.

A person has to understand that there is no carry over from one language to another. You might have had a strong memory in the English language because you memorized songs and poetry. However, in the Arabic language you will be starting from scratch. Work on understanding what you are memorizing, and *insha'Allah*, you will enjoy memorizing much more.

ACTION 2: READING BOOKS OF TAFSEER

This action will require you to complete the first action as a prerequisite. Without the Arabic language, you cannot read books of *Tafseer*. Without reading books of *Tafseer*, you will not fully understand the Quran. You see the importance now.

You can only understand so much of the Quran with your knowledge of the Arabic language. The rest of your understanding must come from reading through all the different books of *Tafseer*.

Where you start with your reading will depend on your knowledge of the Arabic language and your level of knowledge.

If you have a very rudimentary understanding of the Arabic language, I will tell you to start with *Tafseer As-Sa'di*. This *Tafseer* is very basic and is full of beautiful advice from Imam As-Sa'di.

If your level of Arabic is much higher, and you have studied the sciences of the *Deen* a bit, I would tell you to begin with reading *Tafseer Ibn Kathir*. *Tafseer Ibn Kathir* has every science from among the sciences of the Quran in one book while maintaining brevity. If there is an *Ayah* that interprets another *Ayah*, he will bring it. If there is a Hadith which gives the tafseer of an *Ayah*, he will bring it. If an *Ayah* has been abrogated, he will mention it. The only issue with

Tafseer Ibn Kathir is when he goes into issues that people disagree on, a lot of the times he does not give the stronger opinion. He will simply mention the difference of opinion, and then he will go on to the next *Ayah*. To solve this problem, you must sit for a long time with the Ulema.

If your understanding of the Arabic language is really advanced, and you are well-grounded in all the different sciences of the *Deen*, I will tell you to begin with *Adwaa-ul-Bayaan* by Imam Ash-Shinqeeti. This book is a bit advanced but it is absolutely necessary. *Adwaa-ul-Bayaan* is a masterpiece, and it is amazing that it was written in our time. When reading the book, you would think it was written a thousand years ago. This book focuses solely on giving the *Tafseer* of the Quran with the Quran. This book is good to read first before *Tafseer Ibn Kathir* if you are at the level that you can benefit from it. Imam Ash-Shinqeeti was like the Ibn Qutaybah of our time when it came to the Arabic language. The way he would break the language down was excellent. This is a book that all the students that love the Arabic language and *Usool-ul-Fiqh* will enjoy.

Find the level that you fit in, and get started.

Other books which will assist your memorization journey

Tafseer Al-Baghawi: This book is a good companion to keep next to you for a quick reference. In fact, this is one of those reference books which you should always have at arm's length. I mentioned all the different books a student should keep next to him on Telegram, so you will have to search there for that information. Some people would choose *Tafseer Al-Jalaalayn*, but I am not one of those people. *Tafseer Al-Baghawi* has always been my go-to *Tafseer* for quick reference and to prepare for khutbahs and classes. If I feel unsatisfied with what I find in *Tafseer Al-Baghawi*, I will go to *Tafseer Ibn Kathir* to see what he says about the *Ayah*.

Mufradaat Alfaadh-il-Quran: This book was written by Ar-Raaghib Al-Asfahani, and it is another of those books which is absolutely necessary to have by your side. For people who love the language, this is the book for you. Ar-Raaghib breaks down the words and their meanings in the manner they appeared in the Quran. Some words will have different meanings in different contexts, and Ar-Raaghib does a good job at pointing out the different meanings. I have used countless books on the subject of Gharib-ul-Quran in the past, and this book is the one that I found the best of them all. Allah knows best!

Sahih Al-Musnad Min Asbaab-in-Nuzool: This book was written by Imam Muqbil ibn Haadi Al-Wadee'. This book is not a book that you keep by your side as a reference, but it is a book you must read. This book will help you understand the reason certain *Ayaat* were sent down. You can find this information in most books of *Tafseer*, but with this book, you will find the information only from authentic Hadiths, which is very important. Understanding the reason an *Ayah* was sent down helps you understand the *Ayah*. It also gives you a glimpse into the lives of the Prophet ﷺ and his Companions ﷢ at that time.

Tafseer At-Tabari: This book is the king of all the books that have been mentioned. This is the book which you are going to use once you have benefitted from all the previously mentioned books. Once you have a strong understanding of the Quran, you can use this book as a reference book to understand the *Ayaat* of the Quran, and you can also sit down and read it over and over. In fact, to truly benefit from this book, you will have to read it over and over. However, you have to lay the ground work first, and the ground work is laid with the previously mentioned books.

These books are just suggestions based on my experience. There are many other books out there that you might find more beneficial for you, use them. You are not relegated to my suggestions or the suggestions of anybody. You find what works for you and use it.

ACTION 3: LISTENING TO THE QURAN

I have already mentioned this previously, but I will give some detail here that was not given the first time I mentioned it.

First of all, you need to find a reciter that you really jibe with. You want a reciter that recites in a way that you wish to imitate and someone who recites in a correct manner. You do not want to listen to a reciter with a beautiful voice that breaks multiple rules of *tajweed* constantly.

You should stick with one reciter for the time being. In fact, you should keep one reciter that you listen to and one mus'haf that you read from. This will help to etch the Quran into your mind. You will find that when you constantly listen to one reciter, the person's voice gets stuck in your head. You will be reading Quran in *Salat* while the person's voice is playing in your mind. If you read from one *Mus'haf*, you will find that you can visualize the page in front of you when you are reading in the *Salat*.

I would advise you to listen to the Quran whenever you get a chance and you cannot read. If you are driving in the car, working out, cleaning the house, or going to sleep, have something from the Quran playing.

I would also advise you to play the Juz that you are memorizing at night when you are going to bed. Make this the last thing you listen to you before you fall asleep. I take one *Juz* at a time and put it on repeat, so it is the last thing I hear before I sleep and the first thing I hear when I wake up.

For the other activities, I would advise you to use the time to listen to the Quran from beginning to end. If you exercise every day, listen to one *Juz* of the Quran while you are exercising. You will finish listening to the entire Quran once a month. If you are reading the entire Quran once a month also, it will not be long before you find memorization a breeze *insha'Allah*. If you drive back and forth to work every day, you can also use that time to listen to more of the Quran. You might be able to finish the Quran every 15 days if you listen to it at those two times.

I do not generally listen to Quran when I am cleaning the house because I prefer to revise during that time. I like to test myself to see if I can read without making mistakes while doing other activities. If I can wash dishes and read the *Juz* without making a mistake, that means that I truly memorized it.

Again, I cannot stress the importance of only listening to one reciter. I know it sounds difficult, but the reward for doing so trumps the difficulty.

ACTION 4: KEEP A JOURNAL

I know for a lot of men nowadays this suggestion will sound a bit feminine. However, you will have to put your reservations to the side regarding journaling and focus on its benefits.

A journal is not a diary, so you can erase the concept of imitating females. A journal is meant to assist you in being reflective during the process of your memorization. If you do not keep tabs of what works and what does not, how are you going to improve?

For example, you might go out with some friends and eat a certain type of food. Although the food was delicious, you noticed the next day you found a lot of difficulty memorizing. You must make a note of the food you ate the night before and the difficulty you found with memorizing the next day, so you can avoid that problem in the future. You might find that you spend too much time talking with people, so you end up lethargic when it is time to memorize. Make a note of that in your journal and work on fixing the problem. I have found the best way to start finding solutions to a problem is to put the problem into writing. By writing the problem, you are recognizing there is a problem, and then your mind can begin looking for a solution. Otherwise, you will find yourself making the same mistakes over and over again.

Another thing you can include in your journal is miniature experiments and the results you obtained through those experiments.

3. Actions Which Will Assist You During Your Memorization

For example, you might want to see the effects of drinking green tea on the memory. You take 90 days in which you only drink green tea and water. You keep track of your progress to see how your memory improved. You can do the same thing with ginger tea.

You might try new methods of memorization to see if they work. The journal is there to reflect on the results you received from those trials.

There are so many benefits to keeping a journal. However, the journal you keep should only be for your Quran memorization journey. You can have another journal that you write other things in, but you must keep one journal with the sole purpose of keeping record of your journey.

One final benefit of keeping a journal is that you can go back later and visually see your progress. You do not have to rely on your memory to remember how difficult the journey was. If you kept a good record of everything, you will be able to look back on your notes and see the difficulties Allah blessed you to work through. A journal is indispensable.

ACTION 5: FIND A COMPANION TO MEMORIZE AND REVISE WITH

Having a companion that you memorize and revise with is necessary. You must have somebody around you that will catch your mistakes in recitation and motivate you when you get a bit lazy. These two reasons are sufficient to find a person to join you on the journey.

The person does not have to be just two friends. You can memorize Quran with your wife and take her as the companion. You can memorize the Quran with one of your children. You can even memorize the Quran with your parents. It does not matter. What does matter is that the person is serious and ready to put in the work.

How often you recite to the person will depend on your schedule and the schedule of the person you read with. If the person is your wife or child, it is much easier to be more regular with the schedule. If the person is a friend, you might only be able to read together two or three times a week. Whatever you can do, do it. You will find benefit even in one day a week if it is done with consistency.

How much Quran you decided to recite to each other is not important. You can read half of a *Juz*, one *Juz*, two, three, etc. Whatever you have the time for without burning yourself out, do it.

When you are memorizing, you need to find a partner that is on the same level as you or higher. Beware of reading partners that have a lot of mistakes in recitation. If you constantly read with a person that makes a lot of mistakes while you are memorizing, you will begin to pick up their mistakes. It is better for you to read alone if the only person you can find makes mistakes constantly. You also do not want to read with a person that always has an excuse for not revising. People that are not willing to put in the work are a waste of time being around. They stress you out and disappoint you. Again, it is better to read alone.

ACTION 6: WRITING THE QURAN IN NOTEBOOKS

The act of writing nowadays seems to scare people. People have become so accustomed to typing on their electronic devices that I wonder how many people actually still write.

Writing the Quran regularly helps in so many different ways:

First, it gets you accustomed to the style of writing that is found in the *Mus'haf*. Since the *Mus'hafs* that we read from are written in the Uthmani script, is it worth writing the Quran out in that script to become accustomed to it.

Second, writing things out aids greatly in the process of memorization. You literally have to form the words in your mind first before putting the pen to paper. What you see on the paper is produced out of your mind. That is why I always say that it is better for a person to memorize from his own writing than to memorize from a printed book. The same goes for Hadith.

3. Actions Which Will Assist You During Your Memorization

A famous two-line poem expresses this idea:

قيـد صيـودك بالحبـال الواثقـة   العلــم صيــد والكتابــة قيــده

وتركهـا بيـن الخلائـق طالقـة   فمــن الحماقــة أن تصيــد غزالــة

Knowledge is hunted prey, and writing is the rope you tie it down with. Tie up your hunted game with a firm rope. It would be considered stupid for a man to hunt a gazelle, and then leave it untied among creation.

There are different ways that you can write out the *Mus'haf*. You can write out what you memorize little by little. If you take more than one day to memorize a page, you can write the page out every day you take to memorize it. You can also just write out one or two pages per day. By the time you finish writing out the *Mus'haf*, you should be very proficient in the *Uthmani* script. If you do not have enough time to write out one entire page a day, write out half a page, or you can even write out a few *Ayaat* here and there. The whole point is to get you very familiar with the script and writing it out.

ACTION 7: WRITE OUT A DAILY CHECKLIST

I am actually reiterating this point because I went over this in *The Believer's Handbook for Seeking Knowledge.* Having a checklist every day is a must. You will have different tasks that you have to get done every day to attain your ultimate goal, and the easiest way to keep track of those tasks is with a checklist. This checklist should be solely for memorizing the Quran. You can include in the checklist:

- ❍ Your morning reading from the Quran;
- ❍ Your daily reading from *Tafseer*;
- ❍ Your daily repetitions for memorization of the page you are memorizing;
- ❍ Your daily writing task;
- ❍ Your nightly reading from the Quran.

3. Actions Which Will Assist You During Your Memorization

Place the priorities at the beginning of the day and try to get them knocked out early. The more you can get done in the early hours of the day, the less stress you will experience trying to get all the items checked off the list throughout the day.

For some people, it might be a good idea to have a punishment/reward system in place. For example, if you do not check off every item today, you cannot use your phone or laptop at all the next day. You can also punish yourself with push-ups or pull-ups, so you can get a bit stronger in the process. If you manage to check off all the items for the entire week, reward yourself with a large bowl of ice cream on Friday or pizza. You cannot eat the ice cream unless you checked off every item every day.

Do what works best for you.

CHAPTER 4:
The Best Method of Memorization

If you are looking for a definitive answer here, you are going to be highly disappointed. Anybody that is familiar with my previous book, *The Believer's Handbook for Seeking Knowledge,* will know exactly where I am going with this chapter.

The best method of memorization is what works for you. I can only tell you what worked for me, and what worked for me might not help you. I will not go into too much depth in this chapter because I will do that in the next chapter when I speak about the plan *insha'Allah*. For now, let us scratch the surface a bit.

Anybody that knows me, knows that I have been heavily influenced by the method of memorization from Mauritania. I have yet to sit with any students of knowledge that were on their level when it comes to memorization. Throughout my entire time studying, even till today, I will read or listen to anything on the subject of studying in Mauritania. I sat with three Shaykhs from Mauritania in Yemen and Saudi Arabia, and those three, although not strong in their implementation of the *Deen*, were extremely strong in their memories, and that is why I set out to try to learn like them.

The infatuation actually came from a person that studied in Yemen, not Mauritania. By the time I arrived in Atlanta in 1999, I was already accustomed to doing 500 push-ups every other day. This was always my number for push-ups from my days of being locked up. I would do 100 regular push-ups, 100 diamond push-ups, 100 wide push-ups, 100 elevated push-ups, and 100 push-ups on my fingertips. With the

4. The Best Method of Memorization

fingertip push-ups, I would switch between five fingers, three fingers and two fingers.

The brother I met when I was in Atlanta had just returned from Yemen from studying with Imam Muqbil ibn Haadi Al-Waadi'. While he was in Yemen, he studied with a Jordanian brother that had an infatuation with the method of memorization from Mauritania, so he just did what he was told the people of Mauritania did from people he knew who studied there. He found out how much he was able to retain using the method, so he continued on with it. Both of those brothers ended up leaving Yemen and going to study in Mauritania with Shaykh Muhammad Salem Ould Adud in Umm Al-Qura, a village in Mauritania, and both of those brothers, sad to say, are no longer calling to the Sunnah.

When I asked the brother in Atlanta for advice on how to get started memorizing the Quran, he told me, "Just do what the people in Mauritania do." Of course, I asked, "What do they do?" He replied, "They read every page from the Quran they memorize 500 times." When he said that, I just said, "Cool. I already do that with push-ups, so now I will just do it with the Quran." That set the stage for my journey to begin. As I moved around America, I kept that same schedule of memorizing each page by reading it 500 times. I was not memorizing at a quick pace, but what I did memorize stuck. By the time I got to Los Angeles, I was finishing up *Juz Amma*, and I was really hyped. I went on to *Juz 29* by starting with *Surah Al-Mulk*. I finished up *Juz 29* before I left Los Angeles for Texas. Once I finished *Juz 29*, I decided to take the method I was using and try it with *Surah Al-Baqarah*.

By the time I got to Yemen, I had finished the last two *Juz*, *Surah Ar-Rahman*, the first eight pages of *Surah Al-Baqarah* and some other pages I memorized here and there using this method. I was constantly testing my memory by getting up at night for prayer and reciting from different parts I memorized in the *Salat*. In Yemen, I placed all my focus on finishing up *Surah Al-Baqarah*. I wanted to stand up and pray *Surah Al-Baqarah* in one *rakah*, so the only way I could do that was to finish it.

4. The Best Method of Memorization

While I was memorizing *Surah Al-Baqarah*, I was reading it completely almost every day. I was reading each page 500 times, and I read the entire *Surah* about another 200 times by the time I finished memorizing it. At that time, I was able to do what I wanted to do; I stood up and read *Surah Al-Baqarah* in one *rakah* without stuttering. I wish I could say that I could do that now.

For me, there was no doubt that this method of memorization worked. The downside of the method is that it is very time consuming. It is very hard for a person to get up every day and read one page over and over and over. So, this method is not for everybody.

To make counting easy while I was in Dammaj, I asked some brothers to bring me any of the prayer beads they find. I took a piece of wood which was about 15 inches long and placed two nails at the two ends of the board. I ripped the prayer beads off their strings and placed fifty beads on a string attached to the two nails on the board. I would read each page 50 times per sitting. I did not have to keep count anymore because every time I finished reading a page, I would move a bead. Once all the beads were moved over, it was time for breakfast. I would come back after Dhuhr and move them back to the original spot.

Nowadays, I do not need the beads and the board. I use a handheld metal counter. This is much easier and takes up less space. Anybody can buy these on Amazon. You can see an example in the following image:

4. The Best Method of Memorization

Throughout my time in Yemen, I tried different methods, but this is the method that worked best for me. After I finished *Surah Al-Baqarah*, I sat down to see if the method would work on a book like *Al-Usool Ath-Thalathah*. I took about a page at a time and read it 500 times. I would also read the entire *matn* every day while I was memorizing it. By the time I finished, I could read the entire matn from cover to cover without making a mistake. I did the same thing with the Hadiths I memorized and other *mutoon*.

I found another method that also worked well for me, and that involved listening to the *Surah* you are memorizing over and over. Everything about my method of memorization was all about repetition. I had one cassette tape with *Surah Ali Imran* on it. This was recorded in the *Haram* in Ramadan of the year 1420. I only had this tape. I would listen to this tape every night as I was going to sleep. I did that for a long period of time until I finally told myself, "It is time to memorize the *Surah*." I am listening to that same audio right now as I am typing this.

When I began memorizing *Surah Ali Imran*, I noticed how easy it was. I was reading each page about 100 times, and I would be done. I would move to the next page and do the same. That is when I understood that reading something over and over is not the only way to store it in the long-term memory. This discovery for me was groundbreaking. I breezed through the entire *Surah* without a glitch. I still read the *Surah* every day while I was memorizing. I was reading *Surah Al-Baqarah* almost every day, and I would read *Surah Ali Imran*. The Ramadan after I finished *Surah Ali Imran*, I got to test myself once again. I stood up and read *Surah Al-Baqarah* in the first *rakah* without stopping, and I read *Surah Ali Imran* in the second *rakah*. My legs were shot after the first two *rakahs*. I was done, but I felt a sense of accomplishment.

Today, I try to employ all of the methods that helped me. I will listen to the *Juz* I am revising over and over. I will read it once every night while I review the *Juz, Surah-by-Surah*.

As I mentioned, this is what worked for me. You have to find what works for you. Try different techniques and methods, but give

4. The Best Method of Memorization

them time to see if they work. Most people try something for one week, and because they did not see the results they were expecting, they give up and go on to the next method. Try each method 90 days at a time. Use your journal to track your progress. Sometimes, the method is fine, but you have to tweak it a bit to fix your style. If that is the case, tweak it. These methods are not revelation.

In the end, we are all trying to get to the same goal. Whatever method you employ to achieve that goal is not as important as the discipline and consistency you will need to get up every day and do the same thing. Memorizing requires a lot of patience. May Allah make it easy for us!

CHAPTER 5:
Getting Started: The Plan

Now that we have covered the method of memorization, we now have to focus on the next most important issue; making a plan. In any endeavor you wish to undertake, you must have a plan. Success does not happen by accident. A lot of factors go into a person's being successful, and having the correct plan is one of those factors. The most important factor is the *Tawfeeq* from Allah of course. The plan which I am going to detail, *insha'Allah*, is like the method of memorization; it is not set in stone. I can only tell you the plan I had and the methods I employed, and it is up to you to take the information and tweak it to your standards and needs.

This plan is a five-year plan, and I will break it up into different phases. Each phase will have an objective or a certain point you are trying to reach in that phase. I will also begin this plan from a person that is beginning by memorizing *Juz Amma*, which is the 30th *Juz* of the Quran for those that are new. To memorize the Quran in five years, a person must memorize six *Juz* every year. That is one *Juz* every two months, and to do that, you will have to memorize one page every three days. We do have an issue because you will not be memorizing in Ramadan, so you will have to knock out all the memorizing in 11 months. Ramadan is only for reading the Quran during the day and the night.

This plan is for the person who already knows how to read Arabic. If you do not know how to read Arabic, refer back to my previous book *The Believer's Handbook for Seeking Knowledge* because I have a section on the phases of learning the Arabic language. You will find

5. Getting Started: The Plan

what you are looking for in the first phase of the Arabic program.

PHASE 1

This phase begins with memorizing the last three *Juz* from the Quran, and then the plan progresses to the last six *Juz*. The phase will start with *Juz Amma*, and then gradually, you will move on to the next two *Juz* and then the final three. In this phase, life will be simple, so enjoy the simplicity. This phase will take up the first year of memorizing.

When memorizing *Juz Amma*, you have two choices: You can descend from the top or you can ascend from the bottom. My advice is to start from the beginning of the *Juz*, which is *Surah An-Naba*, and ascend. This way, you will knock out all the longer Surahs in the beginning, and the rest will just get easier.

Memorizing *Surah An-Naba* will boost your confidence in the beginning. You might never have thought that you could memorize something that size in the Arabic language, and once you do it, you want to do it more. However, in the end, it is up to you. Start where you feel the most comfortable. When memorizing *Surah An-Naba*, it is a bit confusing because the Surah is a page and a half in length. You have two choices in this scenario: First, you can break the Surah in half, and memorize the first half, the second half, and then read it all together to combine what you memorized. Second, you can just take the entire Surah all at once. That is what I did. Normally, I will not memorize more than a page at a time, but for *Surah An-Naba, Surah An-Naaziaat, Surah Al-Mutafifeen, Surah Al-Fajr* and *Surah Mursilah* I made an exception. In this first part of this phase, your schedule will be very simple. It will look like the following:

Morning	Read *Juz Amma*
Evening	Read the *Surah* you are memorizing and the next one you want to memorize.

5. Getting Started: The Plan

You will memorize throughout the day. Whenever you have free time in the day, pick up the *Mus'haf*, and memorize. Read the *Surah* you are memorizing over and over until you get it. You can set a specific number of times you want to read the page you are memorizing after every *Salat*. For example, after Fajr, read the page 50 times. After Dhuhr, read the page 25 times. After Asr, read the page 25 times. After Maghrib, read the page 25 times. Before going to bed, read the page 15 times. Throughout the day, you would have the page 140 times. If you do that for three days, you will easily memorize a page in that time frame. The best test to know if your memorization of the *Surah* is firm is to recite it as soon as you wake up. If you make any mistakes, keep reading it until you make no mistakes. Another way to test yourself is to read the *Surah* you are memorizing while doing another activity like cleaning or driving (in a safe area of course). If you can do the activity while simultaneously reading the *Surah* from memory without making a mistake, you are good to go.

Once you have finished half of *Juz Amma*, you will add another Juz to your morning reading. You will add *Juz 29* as reading for a second day. Your program will look like the following:

Day 1	
Morning	Read *Juz 29*.
Evening	Read the *Surah* you are memorizing and the next one you want to memorize.

Day 2	
Morning	Read *Juz 30*.
Evening	Read the *Surah* you are memorizing and the next one you want to memorize.

5. Getting Started: The Plan

Once you finish *Juz Amma*, and you are ready to begin *Juz 29*, I advise you to start from *Surah Al-Mulk* and ascend. When memorizing *Surah Al-Mulk* and the succeeding *Surahs*, you can break the *Surah* into two parts and memorize the two parts, one-by-one. Once you finished memorizing the two parts, take two days of reading the entire *Surah* together to keep the flow.

When you arrive at *Surah Nuh*, you will add another day and another *Juz* to your schedule. These earlier phases are for you to build your morning reading plan. Your new plan will now look like the following:

Day 1	
Morning	Read *Juz 28*.
Evening	Read the *Surah* you are memorizing and the next one you want to memorize.

Day 2	
Morning	Read *Juz 29*.
Evening	Read the *Surah* you are memorizing and the next one you want to memorize.

Day 3	
Morning	Read *Juz 30*.
Evening	Read the *Surah* you are memorizing and the next one you want to memorize.

Once you finish *Juz 28*, you will start making bigger jumps. The point

5. Getting Started: The Plan

of beginning simple is to get you accustomed to reading in the morning. Now the program will begin to get a bit more serious.

You will remain on a three-day schedule in regards to the morning reading. However, you will add a *Juz* to be read every day. So, instead of reading one *Juz* a day for three days, you will begin to read two *Juz* a day for three days.

The evening reading will also change. Instead of reading two *Surahs* every night, you will now begin reading the *Juz* that you are memorizing every night. Your new program will look like the following:

Day 1	
Morning	Surah Fusilat to Surah Qaf.
Evening	Surah Adh-Dhariyat to Surah Al-Hadeed.

Day 2	
Morning	Surah Adh-Dhariyat to Surah At-Tahreem.
Evening	Surah Adh-Dhariyat to Surah Al-Hadeed.

Day 3	
Morning	Surah Al-Mulk to Surah An-Nas.
Evening	Surah Adh-Dhariyat to Surah Al-Hadeed.

With this three-day program, you have two choices: First, you can just repeat it over and over, so you finish reading each *Juz* at least 10 times

5. Getting Started: The Plan

a month. Second, you can begin on Saturday and go through the program twice. You will take Jumuah off. On Jumuah, you can just read whatever you want to read.

I would go with the second choice. Use Jumuah to relax and take a break from the schedule because pretty soon, you will not get a day to relax. On Jumuah, you can read whatever you want. If you are a person that sees the recitation of *Surah Al-Kahf* on Jumuah as being authentic, go ahead and do that. You will see, after so many weeks, that you begin to memorize the *Surah* just from reading it every Jumuah.

Once you finish memorizing these six *Juz* of the Quran, you are finished with this phase. At this point, you have memorized one-fifth of the Quran. That is a huge accomplish. Don't get lazy now though because things are going to heat up *insha'Allah*.

PHASE 2

In this phase, you are going to make another jump. You will jump from three days of reading to five days. The point now is to work towards finishing the last ten *Juz* of the Quran. You will begin now from *Surah Ar-Rūm*, and you will read to *Surah An-Nas* every five days. The evening reading will remain the same. This phase will take eight months to complete if you remain on the five-year plan pace. Your new schedule will look like the following:

Day 1	
Morning	*Surah Ar-Rūm* to *Surah Yaseen*.
Evening	Read the entire *Juz* that you are memorizing at the time.

5. Getting Started: The Plan

	Day 2
Morning	Surah As-Saaffaat to Surah Fusilat.
Evening	Read the entire *Juz* that you are memorizing at the time.

	Day 3
Morning	Surah Ash-Shura to Surah Qaf.
Evening	Read the entire *Juz* that you are memorizing at the time.

	Day 4
Morning	Surah Adh-Dhariyat to Surah At-Tahreem.
Evening	Read the entire *Juz* that you are memorizing at the time.

	Day 5
Morning	Surah Al-Mulk to Surah An-Nas.
Evening	Read the entire Juz that you are memorizing at the time.

The day that you read the *Juz* you are memorizing in the morning, you do not have to read it again in the evening. If you want to read it again, that is up to you.

You will continue with this schedule until you are close to finishing these 10 *Juz*. Once you reach around eight and a half *Juz* memorized, you can go on to the next phase *insha'Allah*.

PHASE 3

This phase is going to be exactly the same except you are going to add another day. Instead of a five-day schedule, you will now read for six days. This is the final addition of days. From now on, you will only increase the amount being read per day, not the days. This phase will take four months to complete. Once you are finished with this phase, each successive phase will take a year.

	Day 1
Morning	Surah Al-Furqan to Surah Al-Ankaboot.
Evening	Read the entire *Juz* that you are memorizing at the time.

	Day 2
Morning	Surah Ar-Rūm to Surah Yaseen.
Evening	Read the entire *Juz* that you are memorizing at the time.

	Day 3
Morning	Surah As-Saaffaat to Surah Fusilat.
Evening	Read the entire *Juz* that you are memorizing at the time.

5. Getting Started: The Plan

Day 4	
Morning	Surah Ash-Shura to Surah Qaf.
Evening	Read the entire *Juz* that you are memorizing at the time.

Day 5	
Morning	Surah Adh-Dhariyat to Surah At-Tahreem.
Evening	Read the entire *Juz* that you are memorizing at the time.

Day 6	
Morning	Surah Al-Mulk to Surah An-Nas.
Evening	Read the entire *Juz* that you are memorizing at the time.

Once you finish this phase, you will have finished 12 *Juz* of the Quran. That equates to two-fifths of the Quran. Again, that is a huge accomplishment. You are moving closer and closer to your goal. From the next phase on, you will start to see jumps of six *Juz* per phase.

PHASE 4

This phase, as well as every succeeding phase will have the same set up. You will follow the first schedule for six months, and then you will follow the second schedule for six months. Each six months, you will increase the amount of reading you are doing daily by half a *Juz*, which is 10 pages. This means that every six months, your reading output will increase by three *Juz*.

The First Six Months	
Day 1	
Morning	Surah Al-Kahf to Surah Al-Mu'minoon.
Evening	Read the entire *Juz* that you are memorizing at the time.
Day 2	
Morning	Surah An-Nur to Surah Al-Ankaboot.
Evening	Read the entire *Juz* that you are memorizing at the time.
Day 3	
Morning	Surah Ar-Rūm to Surah As-Saaffat.
Evening	Read the entire *Juz* that you are memorizing at the time.
Day 4	
Morning	Surah Sād to Surah Al-Jathiyah.
Evening	Read the entire *Juz* that you are memorizing at the time.

5. Getting Started: The Plan

Day 5	
Morning	Surah Al-Ah'qaf to Surah As-Saff.
Evening	Read the entire *Juz* that you are memorizing at the time.

Day 6	
Morning	Surah Al-Jumuah to Surah An-Nas.
Evening	Read the entire *Juz* that you are memorizing at the time.

Since this is a six-day schedule, you can take Jumuah off from the reading at night. You should read the *Juz* that you are memorizing every night except that night. However, you will not take a day off from the reading in the morning. As soon as you finish day six, you begin again the next day even if it is a Friday.

The Second Six Months	
Day 1	
Morning	Surah Yusuf to Surah Al-Kahf.
Evening	Read the entire *Juz* that you are memorizing at the time.

5. Getting Started: The Plan

Day 2

Morning	*Surah Maryam* to *Surah An-Nur*.
Evening	Read the entire *Juz* that you are memorizing at the time.

Day 3

Morning	*Surah Al-Furqan* to *Surah Al-Ah'zab*.
Evening	Read the entire *Juz* that you are memorizing at the time.

Day 4

Morning	*Surah Saba* to *Surah Fusilat*.
Evening	Read the entire *Juz* that you are memorizing at the time.

Day 5

Morning	*Surah Ash-Shura* to *Surah Al-Hadeed*.
Evening	Read the entire *Juz* that you are memorizing at the time.

5. Getting Started: The Plan

Day 6

Morning	Surah Al-Mujadilah to Surah An-Nas.
Evening	Read the entire *Juz* that you are memorizing at the time.

At this point, you have completed more than half of the Quran. You will be tempted to begin moving quickly at this point, so you can complete the memorization of the Quran. Don't obey that temptation. Keep this pace. None of us should be in a hurry. We want to memorize the Quran in a firm and strong manner, and you will have to be patient to do that. There are only two more phases to go.

PHASE 5

This phase and the one after it will follow the exact pattern as the previous phase. Each of these phases will take a year.

The First Six Months

Day 1

Morning	Surah Al-An'fal to Surah Ar-Ra'd.
Evening	Read the entire *Juz* that you are memorizing at the time.

5. Getting Started: The Plan

	Day 2
Morning	*Surah Ibrahim* to *Surah Taha*.
Evening	Read the entire *Juz* that you are memorizing at the time.

	Day 3
Morning	*Surah Al-Anbiyyaa* to *Surah Al-Qasas*.
Evening	Read the entire *Juz* that you are memorizing at the time.

	Day 4
Morning	*Surah Al-Ankaboot* to *Surah Sād*.
Evening	Read the entire *Juz* that you are memorizing at the time.

	Day 5
Morning	*Surah Az-Zumr* to *Surah Al-Qamar*.
Evening	Read the entire *Juz* that you are memorizing at the time.

5. Getting Started: The Plan

Day 6

Morning	Surah Ar-Rahman to Surah An-Nas.
Evening	Read the entire *Juz* that you are memorizing at the time.

The Second Six Months

Day 1

Morning	Surah Al-An'am to Surah Surah At-Tawbah.
Evening	Read the entire *Juz* that you are memorizing at the time.

Day 2

Morning	Surah Yunus to Surah An-Nahl.
Evening	Read the entire *Juz* that you are memorizing at the time.

Day 3

Morning	Surah Al-Israa to Surah An-Nur.
Evening	Read the entire *Juz* that you are memorizing at the time.

Day 4

Morning	Surah *Al-Furqan* to Surah *Yaseen*.
Evening	Read the entire *Juz* that you are memorizing at the time.

Day 5

Morning	Surah *As-Saaffat* to Surah *Qaf*.
Evening	Read the entire *Juz* that you are memorizing at the time.

Day 6

Morning	Surah *Adh-Dhariyaat* to Surah *An-Nas*.
Evening	Read the entire *Juz* that you are memorizing at the time.

You have now finished the memorization of four-fifths of the Quran. You are now ready to enter the last and final phase.

PHASE 6

In this phase, we will forego the previous format because you should be ready to read the entire *Mus'haf* every six days. If you feel that five *Juz* every day is too much, you can break the reading up over seven days and read a bit less.

5. Getting Started: The Plan

Day 1

Morning	Surah Al-Fatihah to Surah An-Nisaa.
Evening	Read the entire *Juz* that you are memorizing at the time.

Day 2

Morning	Surah Al-Ma'idah to Surah At-Tawbah.
Evening	Read the entire *Juz* that you are memorizing at the time.

Day 3

Morning	Surah Yunus to Surah Al-Kahf.
Evening	Read the entire *Juz* that you are memorizing at the time.

Day 4

Morning	Surah Maryam to Surah Al-Ankaboot.
Evening	Read the entire *Juz* that you are memorizing at the time.

	Day 5
Morning	Surah Ar-Rūm to Surah Al-Jathiyah.
Evening	Read the entire *Juz* that you are memorizing at the time.

	Day 6
Morning	Surah Al-Ah'qaf to Surah An-Nas.
Evening	Read the entire *Juz* that you are memorizing at the time.

If you follow this schedule for the entire year, you will read the entire Quran at least 60 times. I say "at least 60 times" because you will want to read the Quran more in Ramadan. In fact, you should strive to read ten *Juz* every day in Ramadan.

This is the final phase for memorization. There is, however, another phase which you must complete that is for the purpose of revision and cementing what you have memorized.

PHASE 7

The idea for this phase actually came from a youth that sold vegetables in Dammaj. The beauty of Dammaj was that the farmers and other people of the village used to sit in the classes. I am not saying they were serious Students of Knowledge, but they would sit in the classes and pray with us.

This youth that used to sell vegetables outside the Masjid in Dammaj said that when he finished memorizing the Quran, he took an entire year and read the Quran every three days. He ended up finishing reading the Quran 120 times.

If you cannot read 10 *Juz* a day, read as much as you can. At the very least, continue reading five *Juz* a day for the entire year. You can take one *Juz* to read every night that you are experiencing problems with to fix the problems.

If you do decide to read 10 *Juz* a day, this is what the schedule would look like:

Day 1

Surah Al-Fatihah to *Surah At-Tawbah*.

Day 1

Surah Yunus to *Surah Al-Ankaboot*.

Day 1

Surah Ar-Rūm to *Surah An-Nas*.

If you cannot do this program regularly, try to do it from time to time. You should really try to do it in Ramadan. If you can read 10 *Juz* every day in Ramadan, and you can recite two to three *Juz* every night in prayer, you can finish the Quran 13 times in Ramadan alone.

Keep reading the Quran and keep listening to it. Once you finish memorizing, the task of retaining what you memorized will stick with you until your death.

You should aim to read the Quran at least once a week for the rest of your life. If you get really strapped for time, you can read three *Juz* a day and finish the Quran every 10 days. Do not read less than three *Juz* a day.

The Quran is the most important book you are going to

memorize, so you should not give anything in your life priority over it. The Quran is the priority. Everything else follows the Quran in priority including books of Hadith.

Memorizing the Quran is only the beginning. Now you must seek to understand what you have memorized and act on the knowledge you have. The Prophet ﷺ mentioned in a Hadith in *Sahih Muslim*:

عـن أبي مالك الحـارث بن عـاصم الأشـعري ﷺ قـال : قـال رسـول الله ﷺ: الطهـور شـطر الإيمـان، والحمـد لله تملأ الميزان، وسبحان الله والحمـد لله تملآن ـ أو تملأ ـ مـا بين السماوات والأرض، والـصلاة نـور، والصدقـة برهـان، والصبر ضيـاء، والقرآن حجـة لك أو عليك. كل الناس يغـدو، فبائـع نفسـه فمعتقهـا، أو موبقهـا.

Abu Malik Al-Harith bin Asim Al-Ash'ari ﷺ reported that: The Messenger of Allah ﷺ said: "Purity is half of faith, and the praise of Allah fills the scale. Glorification and praise fill up what is between the heavens and the earth. Prayer is a light, charity is proof of a person's belief, and patience is illumination. The Quran is a proof for you or against you. All people go out early in the morning and sell themselves, either for their freedom or their destruction."

One of the beautiful linguistic aspects of this Hadith is the Prophet's ﷺ using of the word النور and the word الضوء. The word النور in the Arabic language refers to a light that does not produce heat and burning, and the word الضوء refers to a light that produces heat and causes burning. The Prophet ﷺ used the word النور when referring to *Salat* because it acts a source of light for the person in this life and the next without the pain and suffering one has to go through with patience. With patience, you will find heat and burning. The person who remains patient has to endure so much.

The Prophet ﷺ went on to say, "The Quran is a proof for you or against you." The Quran is a proof for the person who reads it, understands it and acts upon it. It is a proof against the person who turns his back on it. He does not read it, he does not care to understand it and he definitely does not act upon it. It is a proof against the person who reads it and understands it, but he does not act on it. We have to strive our entire lives until our deaths in the obedience to Allah in hopes that the Quran will be a proof for us and not against us. May Allah guide us!

CHAPTER 6:
Statements of the Salaf Regarding the Importance of Memorizing and Understanding the Quran

In keeping with my newly found tradition of ending my books with something motivational, I will bring some statements of the people of the past regarding reading and memorizing the Quran.

قال ابن مسعود ﷺ: إن هذه القلوب أوعية فاشغلوها بالقرآن، ولا تشغلوها بغيره.

Ibn Masood ﷺ said, "These hearts are like vessels, so busy you heart with the Quran, and do not busy your heart with anything else."

We do the exact opposite of this advice; we busy our hearts with everything but the Quran. You will even find Students of Knowledge going from one *matn* to another with such energy and fervor, but you will not find the same people displaying the same energy with the Quran. It is sad.

قال عثمان بن عفان ﷺ: لو طهرت قلوبنا، لما شبعت من كلام الله.

Uthman ibn Affan ﷺ said, "If our hearts were pure, we would never tire or become bored with the speech of Allah."

Our hearts are not pure because we are not acting on the first statement. Our hearts are impure because the Quran is not the most important thing to us. May Allah purify our hearts!

ردد الحسن البصري ﷺ ليلة قوله تعالى: ﴿ وإن تعدوا نعمة الله لا تحصوها ﴾ [النحل:18] حتى أصبح، فقيل له في ذلك، فقال: إن فيها معتبراً، ما نرفع طرفاً ولا نرده إلا وقع على نعمة، وما لا نعلمه من نعم الله أكثر.

Al-Hassan Al-Basari ﷺ was standing in night prayer repeating the Ayah (If you were to count the blessings and favors of Allah, you would never be able to count them) until the morning came. Somebody mentioned this action to him, and he responded, "There is a lesson in it. We do not blink our eyes except that we see a blessing when we reopen them, and what we do not know from the blessings and favors Allah has given us is more than what we do know."

عن عبد الله بن مسعود ﷺ قال: ينبغي لحامل القرآن أن يعرف بليله إذا الناس نائمون وبنهاره إذا الناس مفطرون وبحزنه إذا الناس فرحون وببكائه إذا الناس يضحكون وبصمته إذا الناس يخلطون وبخشوعه إذا الناس يختالون. وينبغي لحامل القرآن أن يكون باكيا محزونا حليما حكيما سكيتا ولا ينبغي لحامل القرآن أن يكون جافيا ولا غافلا ولا صخابا ولا صياحا ولا حديدا.

Abdullah Ibn Mas'ood ﷺ said: The person that memorizes the Quran should be known by his nights while the people are sleeping. He should be known by his days while the people are not fasting. He should be known by his sadness while the people are full of joy. He should be known by his crying while the people are laughing. He should be known by his silence while the people are trying to talk over each other. He should be known by his submissiveness to Allah while the people are behaving in an arrogant manner. The person who has memorized the Quran should be crying, stricken with grief (over his past sins), forgiving in times of anger, wise, and extremely quiet. The person who memorized the Quran should not be rough in his manners, heedless, argumentative, loud when he talks and quick to become angry.

I mentioned this statement of Abdullah ibn Masood ﷺ in my first book *The Believer's Handbook for Ramadan*, but it is worthy of being repeated again here.

عن أبي البختري قال: سئل علي بن أبي طالب عن عبد الله بن مسعود ﷺ فقال: قرأ القرآن ثم وقف عنده وكفى به.

Abu Al-Bukhturi said that Ali ibn Abi Taalib was asked about Abdullah ibn Masood ﷺ to which he replied, "He read the Quran, and he implemented it. That is sufficient."

قال سهل التستري ﷺ: علامةُ حبِّ الله، حُبُّ القرآن.

Sahl At-Tusturi ﷺ said, "A sign that a person loves Allah is that he loves the Quran."

قال الإمام ابن كثير ﷺ في تفسير قوله تعالى ﴿إِنَّا أَنزَلْنَاهُ قُرْآنًا عَرَبِيًّا لَّعَلَّكُمْ تَعْقِلُونَ﴾: وذلك لأن لغة العرب أفصح اللغات وأبينها وأوسعها، وأكثرها تأدية للمعاني التي تقوم بالنفوس؛ فلهذا أنزل أشرف الكتب بأشرف اللغات على أشرف الرسل بسفارة أشرف الملائكة، وكان ذلك في أشرف بقاع الأرض وابتدأ إنزاله في أشرف شهور السنة؛ وهو رمضان، فكمل من كل الوجوه.

Imam Ibn Kathir ﷺ mentioned for the interpretation of the statement of Allah (Indeed, We have sent it down as an Arabic Quran, so that you may understand): That is because the Arabic language is the most eloquent of languages, the clearest of languages with the vastest lexis of any language, and the best of all languages in the service of expression for the meanings that lie within the soul. For these reasons, Allah sent down the most noble of books, in the most noble of languages, upon the most noble of Messengers, through the most noble of angels, and this occurred in this most noble of lands of the earth, and it began to be revealed in the most noble of months of the year, which is Ramadan. The Quran is complete from every aspect.

وأوصى الإمام إبراهيم المقدسي تلميذَه عبّاس بن عبد الدايم: أكثر من قراءة القرآن ولا تتركه فإنه يتيسر لك الذي تطلبه على قدر ما تقرأ. قال عباس: فرأيت ذلك وجربته كثيراً فكنت إذا قرأت كثيراً تيسر لي من سماع الحديث وكتابته الكثير وإذا لم أقرأ لم يتيسر لي.

Imam Ibrahim Al-Maqdisi advised his student Abbas ibn Abdi Ad-Daa'im, "Read the Quran a lot, and do not stop reading it because the thing you seek becomes easier as you read the Quran more." Abbas said, "I saw that, and I tried it a lot. I found that if I read the Quran a lot, it became easy for me to hear Hadith and to write a lot of Hadith, and if I did not read the Quran, those things did not become easy for me."

قال ابن مسعود ﷺ: إن العسل فيه شفاء من كل داء, والقرآن شفاء لما في الصدور.

Ibn Masood ﷺ said, "Verily honey is a source of cure for every ailment of the body, and the Quran is the cure for the ailments of the heart.

عن الوليد يعني ابن مسلم قال: كنا إذا جالسنا الأوزاعي فرأى فينا حدثاً, قال: يا غلام, قرأتَ القرآنَ؟ فإن قال: نعم, قال: اقرأ: ﴿يُوصِيكُمُ اللَّهُ فِي أَوْلَادِكُمْ﴾ وإن قال: لا, قال: اذهبْ تعلم القرآن قبل أن تطلب العلم.

Al-Waleed ibn Muslim reported: If we were seated with Al-Awzaa'ee, and he saw among us a young student he would ask him, "Have you memorized the Quran?" If his response was in the affirmative, he would tell him, "Recite 'Allah commands you regarding your children'." If the young student is unable to do so, he will tell him, "Go and learn the Quran before you begin seeking knowledge."

قال شيخ الإسلام بن تيمية في الفتاوى الكبرى: وأما طلب حفظ القرآن فهو مقدم على كثير ما تسميه الناس علماً، وهو إما باطل أو قليل النفع. وهو أيضاً مقدم في التعلم في حق من يريد أن يتعلم علم الدين من الأصول والفروع، فإن المشروع في حق مثل هذا في هذه الأوقات أن يبدأ بحفظ القرآن، فإنه أصل علوم الدين، بخلاف ما يفعله كثير من أهل البدع من الأعاجم وغيرهم، حيث يشتغل أحدهم بشيء من فضول العلم، من الكلام أو الجدال، والخلاف أو الفروع النادرة والتقليد الذي لا يحتاج إليه، أو غرائب الحديث التي لا تثبت ولا ينتفع بها، وكثير من الرياضيات التي لا تقوم بها حجة، ويترك حفظ القرآن الذي هو أهم من ذلك كله.

Shaykh-ul-Islam said in *Al-Fatawa Al-Kubra*: Seeking the memorization of the Quran is a bigger priority than most of what people call knowledge, which is either complete falsehood or the benefit of which is very little. It is also given precedence for the one that wishes to learn knowledge of the *Deen* from foundational knowledge and knowledge that branches off from the foundational knowledge. The one who begins on a journey of knowledge in these days should begin with the memorization of the Quran because it is the foundation of the knowledge of this *Deen*. This is in contrast to what most of the people of innovation from the non-Arabs and other than the non-Arab people of innovation do. They busy themselves with knowledge that does not benefit, such as logic or debate or differences of opinions or rare non-foundational issues of knowledge and blind-following that is not needed. They also focus on searching out and understanding rare speech that is not authentic nor do they benefit from it. They focus on mathematics which no argument could be established upon, and they leave off the memorization of the Quran, which is more important than all that I mentioned.

قال محمد بن الفضل: سمعت جدي يقول: استأذنت أبي في الخروج إلى قتيبة، فقال: اقرأ القرآن أولاً حتى آذن لك، فاستظهرت القرآن، فقال لي: امكث حتى تصلي الختمة، ففعلت،

6. Statements of the Salaf...

فلما عيدنا أذن لي فخرجت إلى مرو.

Muhammad ibn Al-Fadhl said that he heard his grandfather say, "I sought the permission from my father to go study with Qutaybah, and my father told me, 'Memorize the Quran first, then I will give you permission.' So, I memorized the Quran. Then my father said to me, 'Stay until you have recited the entire Quran in the prayer.' So, I did what he told me. While we were celebrating Eid, my father gave me permission to go seek knowledge, so I left to Marw.

This was how the *Salaf* began seeking knowledge; they began seeking knowledge with the Quran first. After the Quran, they would begin memorizing Hadith. During the time they were memorizing Hadith, they would not neglect the Quran.

قال الخطيب البغدادي: ينبغي للطالب أن يبدأ بحفظ كتاب الله عز وجل، إذ كان أجل العلوم وأولاها بالسبق والتقديم.

Al-Khateeb Al-Baghdadi said, "A student should begin with memorizing the Book of Allah because it is the greatest of all the sciences and it has the most right to be the top priority."

قال الإمام النووي ﷺ في مقدمة شرح المهذب: وأول ما يبتدئ به حفظ القرآن العزيز؛ فهو أهم العلوم، وكان السلف لا يعلمون الحديث والفقه إلا لمن حفظ القرآن، وإذا حفظ فليحذر من الاشتغال عنه بالحديث والفقه وغيرهما اشتغالاً يؤدي إلى نسيان شيء منه أو تعريضه للنسيان.

Imam An-Nawawi ﷺ said in the introduction to the explanation of the *Al-Muhadhab*, "The first thing a student should begin with is the memorization of the Quran because it is from the most important of knowledge. The *Salaf* would not teach Hadith or *Fiqh* except to a person who memorized the Quran first. If a student finishes memorizing the Quran, he should beware of becoming distracted with Hadith and *Fiqh* and other sciences that cause him to forget some of the Quran or push him towards forgetting.

I could go on and on from so many different books with so many different statements from the people of the past, but let these statements suffice for now.

We as Americans specifically, and Westerners in general, need to wake up. We are at the bottom of the class when it comes to the Arabic language and memorizing the Quran. People will throw the language excuse around. I would respond to them by saying, "What about the people of Indonesia?" Look at the Indonesians. They do not speak Arabic, yet they have many of their countrymen that have memorized the Quran. They also learn the Arabic language. They go overseas and they are some of the most hardworking students. The complete opposite of the American student of knowledge. The American student of knowledge is the most ignorant of the *Deen* yet the most arrogant. It is a bad mixture. We need to change.

Americans that go overseas to study barely know any Arabic and have memorized very little of the Quran. While Indonesians and Somalis go to study after learning the Arabic language and memorizing the Quran. Pakistanis memorize the Quran in large numbers in America, and they do not speak Arabic. We need to get our act together. We are becoming an embarrassment. We are an embarrassment, but we act like we are God's gift to mankind. We need to wake up and start taking this *Deen* seriously.

We can start taking this *Deen* seriously by becoming serious about learning the Arabic language and memorizing the Quran.

May Allah increase us in knowledge and humility!

CONCLUSION

All praises are due to Allah, who has given us the ability to read His Book, to understand His Book and to act on His Book. We ourselves are the ones that turn our backs on this favor of Allah. May Allah make us grateful for His blessings!

I have laid out, by the permission of Allah, what I amassed in my mind regarding memorization of the Quran. I hope that you, the reader, found ease in understanding every step of the plan. If you found ease and benefit, praise Allah. If you found difficulty in understanding my ideas, ask Allah to forgive my shortcomings.

If you wish to continue memorizing other books after the Quran, such as *Alfiyyah Ibn Malik, Bulugh Al-Maram, Kitab-ut-Tawheed, Al-Aqeedah Al-Waasitiyyah*, or whatever book you wish to memorize, you can employ this same plan.

You only need to read the book in its entirety with a stopwatch running to see how long it takes you to finish the entire book. Once you finish, break the book up into parts and formulate a reading and memorizing plan from there. It is simple. However, I will advise you not to proceed to other books after the Quran until you have truly given the Quran its rights. This is a mistake a lot of us made during our days of studying, and it is a serious mistake. Nothing on the face of this earth deserves our attention more than the Quran, so you do not need to be in a hurry to memorize something else or read something else. While you are memorizing the Quran, you can read books of Hadith, so you do not neglect the understanding of the Sunnah. However, do not make it

Conclusion

a habit of spending hours upon hours reading and memorizing Hadith while you forget the Quran. That is a huge mistake.

May Allah keep us firm on this journey until our souls leave our bodies!

Muhammad ibn James Sutton
Rabi' Ath-Thani 10, 1446 / October 13, 2024
Fresno, California

وَآخِرُ دَعْوَانا أَنِ الْحَمْدُ لِلَّهِ رَبِّ الْعَالَمِينَ

Made in the USA
Middletown, DE
04 November 2024

63457693R00054